The *Will* to *Win*

by

DR. BRIDGET E. HILLIARD

Light Publications
P.O. Box 670167
Houston, Texas 77267

Unless otherwise noted, all Scripture quotations are from the King James Version of the Bible.

ISBN 1-881357-64-3

Printed in the United States of America

Dr. Bridget E. Hilliard

The Will to Win

TABLE OF CONTENTS

Dedication and Thanks 1

Message from the Author 3

Chapter One 7
Understanding the Dynamics of Winning

Chapter Two 13
The Report

Chapter Three 19
The Revelation

Chapter Four 31
The Biblical Principles for Behavior Change

Chapter Five 41
The Power of Your Confessions and Commands

Chapter Six 49
The Principle of Dominant Influence

Chapter Seven 59
The Principle of Accountability

Chapter Eight **63**
The Principle of Saturation

Chapter Nine **69**
Understanding the Will-Setting Process

Chapter Ten **87**
Establishing Your Will

Chapter Eleven **93**
Practical Application of the Willpower Principles

Chapter Twelve **101**
The Seven Steps to Willpower Development

Chapter Thirteen **109**
The Regimentation

Chapter Fourteen **133**
The Rewards

Appendix **141**
FAQs 143
Samples of Pain and Pleasure References 147
Workbook Section 155
Answer Key 169

DEDICATION AND THANKS

I dedicate this book to my partner in life who is my best friend, my mentor, my Pastor, my coach and my #1 motivator, my husband Dr. I.V. Hilliard. Thank you Ira for loving me. You know that only God can love you more than I do. I love you Man!

To my five great and wonderful children in whom I am well pleased. They have become my best friends, my teammates and my overseers (security) for my late nights in the gyms on the road. Thanks Terry and Tina Hilliard-Egans, Jeffery and Irishea Hilliard-Lewis, my precious baby girl Preashea Jewell Hilliard. To my loving precious grandchildren Ira-Emanuel, Briona Janae, Ivan Harrison, and Jonathan Sean Micheal. Thanks for loving grandmommie. I love you all so much.

Thanks Tonya Wilson for being my teammate and pusher in the gym on those early mornings and evenings. You are the "Queen." Keep the will to win. Remember, I am still pushing you. Thanks Victoria "Jazz" for helping me transform my body and using your talents and skills to show me it could be done.

To every member of the Light, 'the church like no other,' you all encouraged me, motivated me and loved me through every step. You inspired me in ways you may never know. I was committed because I knew I wanted to live a long life so that we can continue to build the Kingdom of God together. Thanks New Light Church Houston, Beaumont and Austin. You are indeed a church like no other. I love you.

Finally, to you the reader, thanks for purchasing this book. You have made the first step to Winning in Life. Continue to read and absorb these truths. You have only just begun. Keep the Will to Win!

Dr. Bridget
July 2003

MESSAGE FROM THE AUTHOR

Winning in life is the essence of our human existence. Since God gave Adam the mandate to subdue the earth and have dominion man has possessed the potential to achieve more and perform at higher levels. This book is about winning in life in the area of personal private matters that require discipline, endurance and focus.

In particular, I will be addressing the area of weight loss, but the principles for winning are universal and can be applied to any area of personal struggle. As many will tell you, losing weight is not always an easy accomplishment. It is not always difficult for a lack of discipline or will, but often a lack of information.

Over the years, I have tried a number of weight loss programs and regiments, with some success but never at the level of satisfaction that I desired. The area of discipline and willpower stamina was not a problem because I've learned the principles for establishing the will to succeed which I have applied to other areas of my life. My success in losing over 45 pounds, dropping four dress sizes in three and a half months was the result of both the principles of willpower stamina and the right weight loss program.

The principles set forth in this book will definitely enlighten you to what the Bible says about the will to win. Further, you will be encouraged by the practical examples of the principles I will share. Finally, it is my hope that you will develop a relentless resolve with a renewed passion and purpose to succeed.

This book will be all encompassing starting with my desire to find a weight loss plan that would work for me. Although I didn't have a problem with discipline and willpower to hold a course with a weight loss regiment, so many people I've come in contact with do. A section of this book is devoted to explaining the principle and practice of developing the will and the resolve to be steadfast. If you are serious about winning you will give this section focused attention and absorb the behavior transformation principles. What use is information if you do not have the will to implement the strategy for winning?

I am excited about writing this book more than any book I have authored to date, because I sincerely believe that this will be the catalyst to jump start you on a winning program over your weight or other areas of your life.

What motivates me in life is helping people achieve their goals and dreams. I want you to experience the joy and esteem of success! Taking the time to go through this journey with me will change your life! After living with me through the pages of this book you will never be the same!

Your Partner for the Will to Win!

Dr. Bridget E. Hilliard

The *Will* to *Win*

CHAPTER ONE

UNDERSTANDING THE DYNAMICS OF WINNING

The jeans Dr. Bridget actually wore during her family vacation in December 2002.

UNDERSTANDING THE DYNAMICS OF WINNING

The pursuit of success is always a very personal matter which requires focus, discipline and endurance. We are equipped by God with the potential to raise our productivity and performance through purposeful effort. Behavioral change which equates into performance change is always the product of human effort sustained by divine help. It is through developing a will to win and having an effective strategy for success that goals and dreams can be accomplished.

The major step that must be taken is the mental step of eliminating all excuses for remaining in your present unfulfilled state. **Excuses are the crutches for the uncommitted, and just beyond your excuse is the effort you need to win.** Excuses are the smoke screens of the self deceived! Unfortunately, only you feel your fabricated reason for remaining in your state is justifiable; others who know you know that your flimsy reason is just an excuse.

The next step is gaining the wisdom you need in the area of your success pursuit. In my case I needed wisdom on weight loss principles which included both eating and exercise. It is important to seek out knowledgeable people to access wisdom and refuse to accept myths and misinformation from the uninformed. To win in life you must be willing to invest in the wisdom you need, understanding that a wisdom investment pays off in tremendous dividends that you continue to reap in days to come.

God has uniquely created us as tripartite creatures, body, soul, and spirit. Our success in life is linked inseparably to the development of the soulish area of our lives.

"And the very God of peace sanctify you wholly; and I pray God your whole spirit and soul and body be preserved blameless unto the coming of our Lord Jesus Christ." 1 Thessalonians 5:23

"Beloved, I wish above all things that thou mayest prosper and be in health even as thy soul prospers." 3 John 2

The soul has five components, the mind, the will, the imagination, the emotions and the intellect. You and I will succeed in any endeavor to the degree that we will develop our minds, our wills, our imaginations, our emotions and our intellect. Success and winning then is a product of effort and never occurs by happenstance.

Further, we can do all things within the scope of the will of God and plan of God for our lives through Christ who strengthens us. This in itself is a powerful promise which eliminates the *"I can't"* because the word of God says that you can.

A compelling reason for winning is also critical for establishing a relentless resolve. Looking forward to spoils of the battles is always an incentive and motivation during the difficult times of the journey. **Good health, long life, time with my family and more time to fulfill the ministry assignment on my life are key motivation factors for me and ultimately define my compelling "why" in my quest to win the battle over my weight.** Your compelling reason becomes the anchor for your resolve and keeps you stable during the stormy times during the journey.

Choosing not to hide behind excuses and being armed with the promise of God to help us win, with knowledge that wisdom for winning is essential, and a compelling reason for winning. We are ready for the pursuit!

The *Will* to *Win*

CHAPTER TWO

THE REPORT

The Will to Win

Dr. Bridget–July 2002

THE REPORT

It is does not take a genius mentality to understand the advantages of weight control. Newspaper articles, television programs along with doctors are all preaching the same message of how weight loss can significantly improve your health. Without being redundant with information that we have already been overdosed on, let me use this chapter of the book to remind you of the tremendous health advantages in weight loss and management.

Almost 65% of people in the US are either overweight or obese. Overweight is defined a roughly 10-30 pounds over a healthy weight; obesity is 30 or more pounds over. People who weigh too much are at an increased risk of heart disease, diabetes, many types of cancers and other illnesses. *US Today Information Network–May 14, 2003*

My desire to lose weight was really multi-faceted. First of all, I am a very health-conscious person and I understand that you cannot expect good healthy living in violation of healthy principles. Secondly, I love to look good in the latest fashions, which many times are not as plentiful in the larger sizes. My third desire is that I am conscious that my family genes lean toward obesity, therefore I must exercise discipline in this area.

After trying multiple programs and yet not experiencing the kind of lasting results I was seeking, I was stimulated in my search for a workable plan by the report from my annual health check up. When I received the results, the blood work showed that my cholesterol was getting dangerously high. I could hardly believe this because my normal eating pattern was what most people would call healthy. Everything always in moderation, coupled with exercise, I really thought all was well. The doctor suggested that I lose 30 lbs to bring the cholesterol down. This weight loss would prevent me from taking medication to control a potential cholesterol problem.

In the meanwhile, my doctor provided me with a suggested diet plan and some suggested medicine that would help regulate cholesterol. Of course you know that most medicines have serious side effects associated with them, and long-term use could be counter productive to your health. I knew that I had to do something to get on track for good health and to stay on track. It was obvious that the information and the present exercise regiment was not working for me, I needed to get wisdom from knowledgeable sources to develop a new strategy for my life.

After much prayerful consideration I was inspired by the Spirit of God to get a personal trainer, it seemed good to me because this was the only weight loss regiment I had not done. I remembered one of our church members who was a personal trainer who had worked with several members of the church who were pleased with the results. I contacted her and talked the matter over with my husband and my children. The children were excited about the idea of having a trainer so we decided to pursue this course of action and we are so glad that we did.

I know that many of you who are reading this book may feel that you cannot afford a trainer and therefore the rest of this story is irrelevant, but it's not. Continue to read on and you will discover, like we did, and the scripture validated that **bodily exercise is not the main factor, it attributes to about 20% of your success–proper eating contributes the other 80%.** Our trainer, who you will hear from later in this book, directed us to a nutritionist who had proven results with her clients, and this component was an important link in the process. In a later chapter, my trainer will share the exercise program she designed for me and I will share what the nutritionist instructed me to do.

Now that we are on track with the physical components of the strategy, let me bring you up to date with the spiritual and mental toughness and will to win necessary to achieve success. As you know, many people have exercise equipment and have been instructed in proper eating, but the fallout many times is not in a lack of knowledge, but in a lack of disciplined will to start and stick with a proven plan of action until success is achieved. This next chapter and the wisdom I will be sharing will change your life forever! Get ready to Win!

CHAPTER THREE

THE REVELATION

The *Will* to *Win*

Dr. Bridget–February 2000

THE REVELATION

This chapter of the book is to instruct you in developing the discipline necessary to follow through on your commitment to a winning strategy. The truths I am about to share with you are truths that I have watched change the lives of thousands in our local church in Houston. It will be beneficial to read this chapter several times and allow this information to permeate your spirit and soul. We are about to take a journey into the mechanics of renewing the mind and setting the will to win in life.

What is so incredible about this chapter is that these principles are so powerful that they will work in any endeavor. They are extracted from the word of God and made practical and applicable so that you will experience success like never before.

"I can do all things through Christ which strengtheneth me." Philippians 4:13

Winning over the critical challenges in life is the hallmark of the Christian way of life. Winning is the aggressive focused pursuit and attainment of worthy goals by functioning with excellence by overcoming obstacles and developing one's potential.

Winning the personal battles of life will cause you to experience a higher quality of life, however, this only occurs when you develop the skills and discipline necessary to execute a well conceptualized program. I come in contact with people all the time who are struggling and fighting seemingly losing battles with unhealthy habits, procrastination, unwanted pounds and inches, addiction to legal and illegal drugs, and the lack of discipline and constant emotional pain that undermines confidence and self-esteem.

From God's Word, my husband and I have developed a simple program that equips believers with the tools and skills to develop and mobilize their ability to overcome bad habits and to enjoy a greater degree of success. At the root of excellence in performance and discipline is the power of the human will to exert control over self-defeating habits.

Our research and study over the years has uncovered that the primary element controlling human behavior change is the will of man. The will of man is the "thermostat of life." **Once the thermostat of life, which is the will, is set, all internal processes are set in motion to accomplish the will's desire.** Contrary to popular opinion, taking charge of your will is not as difficult as you think. It is your responsibility to harness your will and direct it so that it works for your benefit. It can set your life on a new course when you learn to take charge of your will.

Understanding the Power of the Human Will

Understanding the will of man requires some simple insight into God's creative design for mankind. The Word of God is the primary source for explanations regarding the nature of mankind. The Bible explains how God designed the human mind and how we are to properly manage our human behavior and our interpersonal relationships. It is refreshing to know that God cared about man's mental and emotional well being enough to give insight into human behavior in advance of the emergence of the fields of psychiatry and psychology.

Key Statement: The will of man is the most dominant authority over human affairs in the earth.

The will of man is the primary factor in the control of human affairs, and must be respected as such, since even God will not violate a man's will. God will not save a man against his will and contrary to what most people think Satan cannot make a person do anything against his will.

The Tripartite Nature of Man

God has uniquely created man as a tripartite being. According to ***1 Thessalonians 5:23,*** man has a spirit, soul, and body. More accurately, man is a spirit, he lives in a body, and he possesses a soul. There are five components of the soul: the mind, the will, the imagination, the emotions, and the intellect. The Word of God instructs us that we will do well in life (prosper) and be in health relative to the development of the soul ***(3 John 2).***

The Importance of the Will of Man

During my intensive study of this years ago I was so amazed at the number of things that are affected by the will of man. These things are revealed as you examine principles that are taught and different examples where the will of man is involved. The will of man controls the following:

- The degree of obedience - obedience is always a matter of conscious effort on our part regulated by our human wills

- The level of believing - believing at any level is subject to what the individual is willing to accept as believable

• The power fear has over us - fear is only effective to the degree that a person is willing to yield themselves to the potential danger the situation suggests

• The consistency of our character - the consistency of our behavior is subject to our willingness to function according the values and core beliefs

• The measure of blessing we enjoy in life- the quality of life we experience is subject to our willingness to pursue what we have defined as quality of life.

Life is choice driven. We live or die by the choices we make. The quality of life that is promised in the scriptures for the believer does not automatically come to pass. A person must be willing to follow Godly principles to experience the promises of the scriptures.

Key Statement: Establishing your will is your responsibility, not God's.

The story of Thomas, found in the Gospel of John, provides exciting insight into the establishing of the human will.

"But Thomas, one of the twelve, called Didymus, was not with them when Jesus came. The other disciples therefore said unto him, We have seen the Lord. But he said unto them, Except I shall see in his hands the print of the nails, and put my finger into the print of the nails, and thrust my hand into his side, I will not believe." John 20:24-25

Thomas was basically saying that if he was going to set his will to believe that Jesus was resurrected from the dead, he needed to personally examine the body of Jesus. Thomas' honesty gives us insight into how we function psychologically. Thomas' criterion for setting his will to believe was a hands-on, personal examination of Jesus. Each of us have different requirements that must be satisfied before we set our will to believe anything!

Jesus appeared eight days later and allowed Thomas to examine Him based on Thomas' criterion. Jesus then said something that gives us incredible insight into the systematic way that man functions. Jesus turned from Thomas and said, ***"Blessed are they that have not seen and yet have believed."*** Jesus challenged Thomas to change the basis on which he established his thinking. Jesus says blessed are they that have believed and have not seen. Blessed means empowered to prosper, to succeed, to win. Therefore, Jesus is saying that those who have not seen and yet are able to set their will to believe are empowered to prosper and win in life. Jesus' statement also means that we have the power to redefine the criteria for establishing our will to believe. Since I have the power to change the criteria, I am in control of my will and I am not and do not have to be a victim of how my will is presently dysfunctioning relative to my goals.

Jesus was able to say this because He knew what He had done in the Garden of Gethsemane. He reversed what Adam had done in the Garden of Eden. When Adam ate the fruit from the tree of the knowledge of good and evil, he was essentially saying Not your will Lord, but my will be done. When we place our will above God's Will for us, then we subject ourselves to the controlling influence of satan. In the Garden of Gethsemane, Jesus said, ***"Not my will but thine will be done." Luke 22:41-44*** says, ***"And he was withdrawn from them about a stone's cast, and kneeled down, and prayed, Saying, Father, if thou be willing, remove this cup from me: nevertheless not my will, but thine, be done. And there appeared an angel unto him from heaven, strengthening him. And being in an agony he prayed more earnestly: and his sweat was as it were great drops of blood falling down to the ground."***

Herein lies an astounding life-changing truth. When we set our wills in agreement with God's will for our lives with a commitment to pursue his plan at all cost, we are spiritually strengthened for the journey. Just as the angel appeared to help Jesus in his pursuit of God's plan for His life, you and I can depend on heavenly strength to help us in every God pleasing endeavor. Thus this capsulated statement, **change for the believer is a product of human effort sustained and strengthened by divine help.** The apostle, Paul, writes this comforting passage further validating this truth:

"That he would grant you, according to the riches of his glory, to be strengthened with might by his Spirit in the inner man;" Ephesians 3:16

Key Statement: Change is always the product of human effort.

One of the most astounding truths that you and I must embrace is that change is the product of human effort and is sustained by divine help. Many Christians live under the misguided expectation that God is going to somehow supernaturally change their desires and actions at a twinkling of an eye and they will be free of self-defeating habits and embarrassing misbehavior. I do not deny that a miracle of this nature is not possible, but miracles are not within our control and cannot be predicted.

The new birth does not change the body or the mind. According to the Bible, the new birth is a spiritual transaction that changes the spirit of man. The new birth experience also raises the level of man's desire for the things of God and starts the real work of lifestyle transformation.

"I beseech you therefore, brethren, by the mercies of God, that ye present your bodies a living sacrifice, holy, acceptable unto God, which is your reasonable service. And be not conformed to this world: but be ye transformed by the renewing of your mind, that ye may prove what is that good, and acceptable, and perfect, will of God. For I say, through the grace given unto me, to every man that is among you, not to think of himself more highly than he ought to think; but to think soberly, according as God hath dealt to every man the measure of faith." Romans 12:1-3

"Set your affection on things above, not on things on the earth." Colossians 3:2

According to these scriptures, it is my responsibility to do something with my body, my mind, and my affections.

In the Garden of Gethsemane when Jesus purposed to drink from the cup, to fulfill God's will for his life, angels came to strengthen him. When we put forth the effort needed for change, we can be assured that our initiative will be assisted and supported by God. We will also experience a spiritual strengthening that will help us to stay on course. You must want to change and you must be willing to produce those changes that you desire. You must put forth the effort to obtain your desire whether that desire is to lose weight, to stop smoking, to eliminate procrastination, to set worthwhile goals, or to develop better discipline for greater levels of excellence. Whatever your desire, whatever is the object of your affection that is not contrary to the Word of God, you will learn in the following pages how to put forth the proper effort for behavioral change that is in agreement with the scriptural principles for behavioral change.

CHAPTER FOUR

THE BIBLICAL PRINCIPLES FOR BEHAVIOR CHANGE

The *Will* to *Win*

THE BIBLICAL PRINCIPLES FOR BEHAVIOR CHANGE

There is a wealth of knowledge concerning behavioral change in the Bible. My husband and I have used the following principles in our local church to minister life-changing strategies to our membership struggling with dysfunctional behavior. We have seen so many people overcome life's challenges through these effective principles–from ministering to drug addicts to those struggling with their weight, to couples dealing with marital problems, and to businessmen needing to overcome procrastination to gain a competitive edge in business.

The most stable chairs are supported by four legs. It has been proven that four legged support provides very good, dependable and durable support system. The behavior transformation strategy is based on the following four simple, but dynamic, principles that, once learned and implemented, sets life on a winning course.

- The Principle of Faith Confessions
- The Principle of Dominant Influence and Modeling

- The Principle of Accountability
- The Principle of Saturation

The Principle of Faith Confessions

The Will of God is not automatic. The Bible teaches that God needs our permission and our participation for Him to move into our affairs. Faith releases the Power of God. We must release our faith to allow God to move into our personal day-to-day affairs. Faith is more than simply believing that God has the power to do something–God's Power to act is never in question. Faith is the ability to move the Hand of God into our situations based on what He promises to do in His Word. Therefore, we must become familiar with His Word by reading, studying, digesting, and applying the Word everyday.

Mark 11:24 says, ***"Therefore I say unto you, What things soever ye desire, when ye pray, believe that ye receive them, and ye shall have them."*** This is biblical believing. Biblical believing is accepting as fact that for which you have no sense realm evidence–in other words, you cannot see, hear, feel, smell, nor touch that which you choose to accept as a fact. The Word of God tells us that there is more to life than what we perceive with our physical senses. ***Colossians 1:16*** states: ***"For by him***

were all things created, that are in heaven, and that are in earth, visible and invisible." You may be seeking some things that are invisible to you now. You may want or need discipline in your eating and exercise habits, you may want or need freedom from smoking, drug abuse, and procrastination, or you may want discipline for excellence. Since ***Ephesians 1:3*** says, ***"Blessed be the God and Father of our Lord Jesus Christ, who hath blessed us with all spiritual blessings in heavenly places in Christ,"*** all these things are already ours in the spirit realm. They are just waiting for us to release our faith to receive them.

Remember that faith is the substance of things hoped for, the evidence of things not seen. We see the unseen through the Word of God. The Word of God is our evidence. The Word of God serves as our spiritual telescope that enables us to see the Promises and Principles that God has already spiritually prepared for our use. Believing the Promises and Principles of the Word is a matter of your will. You can choose to believe or you can choose not to believe. We saw an example of this in ***John 20:24-28*** in the life of Thomas.

After salvation, faith is the most important lesson for the believer to learn. This is critically true for several reasons. One reason faith is so important is that it pleases God and He will reward those who diligently seek Him by faith. ***Hebrews 11:6*** says, ***"But without faith it is impossible to please him: for he that cometh to God must believe that he is, and that he is a rewarder of them that diligently seek him."***

Another reason faith is so important is that all of the promises of God are received by faith. If I am to receive the promises of God, I must have faith. ***Galatians 3:13-14*** says, ***"Christ hath redeemed us from the curse of the law, being made a curse for us: for it is written, Cursed is every one that hangeth on a tree: That the blessing of Abraham might come on the Gentiles through Jesus Christ; that we might receive the promise of the Spirit through faith."*** Although this passage is talking about the promise of the Holy Spirit, this is how all the promises of God are received.

A third reason faith is important in the life of a believer is that faith enables you to overcome any situation. Your commitment to the principle of faith determines whether you will be a victim of your circumstances or a victor over your circumstances.

"For whatsoever is born of God overcometh the world: and this is the victory that overcometh the world, even our faith." 1 John 5:4

Since faith is so important, you are probably asking yourself: How do I get it and how do I increase it? When we are born again, our spirit becomes alive to the things of God and at that moment God deposits faith into our hearts.

"For I say, through the grace given unto me, to every man that is among you, not to think of himself more highly than he ought to think; but to think soberly, according as God hath dealt to every man the measure of faith." Romans 12:3

God gives us the measure of faith, but it is our responsibility to develop or increase the measure that we have. What you and I receive from God and what we are able to overcome in life will be determined by the development of our faith.

"So then faith cometh by hearing, and hearing by the Word of God." Romans 10:17

To increase my faith I must increase my intake of the Word of God.

There are two things that are essential to the God Kind of Faith:

- The Word of God and
- What you do with the Word of God.

You cannot have faith apart from the Word of God.

"And this is the confidence that we have in him, that, if we ask any thing according to his will, he heareth us: And if we know that he hear us, whatsoever we ask, we know that we have the petitions that we desired of him." 1 John 5:14-15

Faith starts where the Will of God is known and the Will of God is found in the Word of God. ***Colossians 1:9-10*** states, ***"For this cause we also, since the day we heard it, do not cease to pray for you, and to desire that ye might be filled with the knowledge of his will in all wisdom and spiritual understanding; That ye might walk worthy of the Lord unto all pleasing, being fruitful in every good work, and increasing in the knowledge of God."*** You cannot release faith for that for which you have no knowledge.

Listening to the Word of God is crucial to the development of faith. Since ***Romans 10:17*** tells us that ***"So then faith cometh by hearing, and hearing by the Word of God,"*** you have to make it a point to listen to the Word of God everyday. Notice that that scripture did not say that faith comes after you have heard the Word of God. The scripture states that faith comes by hearing and hearing. Therefore, it is very important to listen to the Word of God continuously.

The Word must be spoken just as God did in the first chapter of Genesis. God changed the world by speaking it into existence. ***Hebrews 11:3*** says, "***Through faith we understand that the worlds were framed by the Word of God, so that things which are seen were not made of things which do appear.***" We see the earth void and without form in Genesis 1:2, but we see God speaking it into existence in the next few verses. The psalmist says in ***Psalms 33:6-9, "By the word of the LORD were the heavens made; and all the host of them by the breath of his mouth. He gathereth the waters of the sea together as an heap: he layeth up the depth in storehouses. Let all the earth fear the LORD: let all the inhabitants of the world stand in awe of him. For he spake, and it was done; he commanded, and it stood fast.***"

There are many blessings of God that are void and without form in your life. You must speak them into existence just as God did. You are made in His image and likeness. He has given you the authority to change your world.

Faith is released by the words of our mouth. The Bible teaches in ***Mark 11:23-24*** that we will have what we say. A perfect example of faith being released by the spoken word is seen in the experience of Jesus and His disciples while they were at sea in a life-threatening storm. The disciples were fearful for their lives. They went to Jesus, who was asleep in the boat, and declared to Him their impossible situation. Jesus stood and spoke to the winds and the waves saying, "Peace Be Still." There was a great calm. Then He turned to the Disciples and said to them, "Where is your faith?" In other words, they could have released their faith for deliverance in the same manner that Jesus had released His faith.

Chapter Five

The Power of Your Confessions and Commands

The *Will* to *Win*

THE POWER OF YOUR CONFESSIONS AND COMMANDS

The word *confession* in the Christian community has several connotations. One common meaning is that of acknowledging your sins to a priest. This is not what is meant in the context of this book and teaching on faith. **A confession is a verbal affirmation of scriptural truth about a situation. A faith confession is a statement in agreement with what the Word of God says about a situation regardless of what that situation appears to be. Romans 10:10** teaches that with the heart we believe and with the mouth we confess. The word *confess* comes from a Greek word that means *to say in agreement with or to say the same thing as.* The Principle of Faith Confession says basically that I must choose by an act of my will to agree with God and His Word and speak forth that agreement. When I choose God's Word for my lips, I choose His Will for my life.

"I call heaven and earth to record this day against you, that I have set before you life and death, blessing and cursing: therefore choose life, that both thou and thy seed may live." Deuteronomy 30:19

Life is what I want and I presume life is what you want, so how do we choose it? How do we get it? How do we get life? According to ***Proverbs 18:21, Death and life are in the power of the tongue: and they that love it shall eat the fruit thereof."*** Couple this with ***John 6:63*** which states that the Word of God is life. We can then see that we can choose life with what we choose to say. Police the words of your mouth because what you say will one day be your prison. Consider ***Proverbs 6:2: "Thou art snared with the words of thy mouth, thou art taken with the words of thy mouth."*** Life is in the power of your tongue.

There are several reasons that we would want to ascribe to faith confessions. One is that **your faith is made effective by acknowledging every good thing that you have in Christ Jesus.** Therefore, you should only allow the things you have in Christ Jesus to come out of your mouth. How do you do that? Start calling those things that are not as though they were. ***Romans 4:17*** says, ***(As it is written, I have made thee a father of many nations,) before him whom he believed, even God, who quickeneth the dead, and calleth those things which be not as though they were.***

Another reason a faith confession is important is found in ***Isaiah 55:10-11.*** It states, **The Word of God will never return unto Him void, but we must send His Word out.**

"For as the rain cometh down, and the snow from heaven, and returneth not thither, but watereth the earth, and maketh it bring forth and bud, that it may give seed to the sower, and bread to the eater: So shall my word be that goeth forth out of my mouth: it shall not return unto me void, but it shall accomplish that which I please, and it shall prosper in the thing whereto I sent it." Isaiah 55:10-11

God's Word has to do what it is sent to do. It cannot return to Him without performing as it should.

The third reason why a faith confession is important is the fact that **God creates the fruit of our lips.** In other words, He creates what I say. ***Isaiah 57:19*** tells us that He creates the fruit of the lips. Therefore, we should say what we want Him to create.

A fourth reason for a faith confession is found in ***Mark 11:23,*** which states, ***"For verily I say unto you, That whosoever shall say unto this mountain, Be thou removed, and be thou cast into the sea; and shall not doubt in his heart, but shall believe that those things which he saith shall come to pass; he shall have whatsoever he saith."*** The **"shall having"** mentioned in this verse **depends on what I say.**

A faith command is the essence of "Self Talk" and different from a faith confession. A faith confession is a statement about what God's word says about situations, whereas, a faith command is the believers authority to speak change to situations. In ***Mark 11:23,*** Jesus said to say unto the mountain. On another occasion in ***Luke 18:2,*** Jesus said to speak to the tree and it should obey you. A faith command is speaking to a thing with spiritual authority.

A good example of these two principles in action would be making a statement about God's will for you to eat healthy and live a long life. Making a faith confession would sound something like this:

> "Father, I thank you that your Word says that I should desire those things that are beneficial to my body and exercise discipline and discretion in my eating selection. I eat only those things that are healthy and beneficial and only enough for my satisfaction and never as a glutton."

Now, a faith command would speak to the body and not about the resolve you have in the situation. A faith command would be fashioned something like this:

> "Body, I now exercise discipline and control over you and I command you to desire only those things that are healthy and beneficial.

> You will only eat with discretion and discipline, only eating what is sufficient."

This will become very helpful for you on those days when your body does not feel like carrying out the weight control strategy of either eating or exercise. During those times you must exercise these principles of confession and command in order to stay the course to get the winning results.

Dr. Bridget–New Year's Eve 2000

CHAPTER SIX

THE PRINCIPLE OF DOMINANT INFLUENCE

The *Will* to *Win*

THE PRINCIPLE OF DOMINANT INFLUENCE

What I am now about to share with you is a simple principle but it is probably one of the most important components relative to behavior change. The Principle of Dominant Influence is about controlling influences that significant others have upon our behaviors and habits. As we attempt to change behavior patterns and break poor habits, we must recognize the impact others (whom we consider to be important to us) have on us. Our human need for acceptance is a power motivator. The people with whom you interact will have an impact either negatively or positively upon your success.

Dr. Bridget–January 2003

The Bible teaches that the wise person

carefully evaluates his/her relationships to determine whether or not they are beneficial and worthwhile. ***Galatians 5:7-9*** says, ***"Ye did run well; who did hinder you that ye should not obey the truth?"*** This persuasion cometh not of him that calleth you. A little leaven leaveneth the whole lump. It is critical that you keep yourself in an environment that will support you in your pursuit of success. You do not need negative influences.

Whoever is exerting the most dominate influence on your life is directing you either toward your destiny or away from your destiny. You can often look and listen to them to decide the direction of the pull. Influence is the power to affect the decisions, values and behavior of others through subtle, but impactful means. No matter how powerful the influence, it is still subject to the will of the person. ***Psalms 1:1-3*** testifies of our control of the amount of influence others have over us.

"Blessed is the man that walketh not in the counsel of the ungodly, nor standeth in the way of the sinners, nor sitteth in the seat of the scornful. But his delight is in the law of the Lord; and in his law doth he meditate day and night. And he shall be like a tree planted by the rivers of water, that bringeth forth his fruit in his season; his leaf also shall not wither; and whatsoever he doeth shall prosper." Psalms 1:1-3

To achieve any goal or dream, you must carefully manage the circle of influence you have around you. The real level of commitment you have to any task or objective is clearly seen in the types of influences you allow relative to that objective or task. Believers are instructed not to become unequally yoked with unbelievers because of its negative effect.

14 "Be ye not unequally yoked together with unbelievers: for what fellowship hath righteousness with unrighteousness? and what communion hath light with darkness?"
17 "Wherefore come out from among them, and be ye separate, saith the Lord, and touch not the unclean thing; and I will receive you." 2 Corinthians 6:14,17

Influence is not always a blatant intrusive force, but normally a subtle persuasive or coercion, which must be permitted and can always be resisted.

Hebrews 6:12 goes further to say, ***"That ye be not slothful, but followers of them who through faith and patience inherit the promises."*** This may call for making adjustments in relationships that are not supportive of your goals until you have developed the discipline to stay on course with your plan. Those persons who will discourage you and even tempt you to abandon your goal should not occupy major parts of your time. Find those who are pursuing similar goals and link up with them.

It is this principle that "support groups" are based on. I was so very fortunate in this weight loss and healthy life pursuit because we were able to make it a family affair. The loving support of those close to you who you love and need acceptance from is important for an enjoyable atmosphere during the journey. Even though my husband did not participate in the exercise regiment or eating program, his commitment to a weight management and eating regiment that works for him is equally inspiring.

Natural development is always accelerated through a visible natural example. Therefore, there are two things that you should do to help ensure your success. The first thing you should do is to eliminate sucker relationships. These are people who pour cold water on your dreams, ideas, and faith.

Second Corinthians 6:14 is instructive here: ***"Be ye not unequally yoked together with unbelievers: for what fellowship hath righteousness with unrighteousness? and what communion hath light with darkness?"*** If you happen to be in an existing relationship with this type of person (sucker), for instance, if you are married to a person who tends to always douse your dreams, ideas, and faith walk with negative commentaries and actions, please remember that you have the Grace of God to handle the relationship. In this situation it is best to pray and seek ways to communicate your need for their support. I have discovered that many times those around us are not aware of the negative things they do to hinder us.

The second thing you should do is to develop relationships with people who are growing and going especially in common areas. These are people who are growing in the things of God such as understanding His Will, His Word, and His Way, and are going toward their increasing levels of excellence, satisfaction, and esteem. Establish a relationship with others who are going somewhere. It is okay to have a relationship with those who are not where you are presently if they want to do better. You and I are responsible to help and aide others in their success. You will readily identify these persons because they will respond positively to your attempts to pull them to higher levels of productivity. ***Second Corinthians 3:2*** says, ***"Ye are our epistle written in our hearts, known and read of all men." Luke 22:32*** tells us that we should strengthen the brethren. It is also necessary and very worthwhile to have relationships with those who have surpassed where you are. These relationships will also inspire, push, and pull you to do better.

The most practical respect for the principle of influence is seen in the selection of a role model. A role model is one who provides a visible natural example of that which is desired. Jesus is our role model. He did as the Father commanded. We can see the positive proof that if we follow Christ as He followed the Father, we will be victorious in all that we set our hands to do according to His Will and ultimately please the Father as well. Having a role model helps you to stay on target with what you want to accomplish in life.

We should also model the growth strategies of successful others. It is the order of God to teach us and to train us by examples. You want to find a successful individual who has succeeded in what you want to do and you should use that person as a model. You are going to model the growth strategy that your role model used because principles work for anybody who will work them. ***Hebrews 6:12*** says, ***"That ye be not slothful, but followers of them who through faith and patience inherit the promises."*** The word *followers* used in this scripture is the same as the word *imitators*. Therefore, the Word of God instructs us to be imitators of those who are successful.

Without boasting, my husband and I are considered as very successful. I assist my husband in the leadership of our incredible church which started with 23 members and now numbers over 24,000. We attribute our growth, success and excellence in ministry to God and the influence of the role model we embraced. Drs. Fred and Betty Price, of the Crenshaw Christian Center Church of Los Angeles, California became our role models years ago when our church was very small. We modeled their ministrie's policies and procedures, maintained our own personalities as we imitated the growth strategies of these two wonderful successful people. These people became mentors to us and we sought the deposits that they could and did make in our lives. The principles that have worked for them have also worked for us.

Your mentor does not have to be your buddy. You can be mentored from afar. In some cases, your mentor may not even know you. What you want from the mentor is the visible example of their success and the road map they used to get there. Often times you can get these two elements without a close intimate relationship, but can glean these from their teaching tapes, books or biographies. There is no need to be ashamed of the mentoring process. Being mentored does not mean that you are not your own man. As a person being mentored, you tap into the pattern of success of a person by becoming a student of that person with regards to how they handle certain situations or deal with certain challenges.

There is a natural progression in the development of a mentoring relationship. At the first stage you become an admirer. This person appreciates the mentor from a distance and is attracted by the mentor's lifestyle. At the next stage, you become a distant disciple. Disciples aggressively embrace the principles and concepts that produced the lifestyle that is modeled by the mentor. At the final stage you become a supporter of your mentor. This is a person who chooses to embrace the passion and vision of their mentor with a calculated commitment to help them accomplish theirs goals. This is the level at which the mentoring relationship is mutually beneficial.

Although a role model is helpful, it is not essential. There are those who have achieved tremendous success as pioneers in their various fields. So if you cannot readily identify a role model don't be discouraged. The principles for winning will work for you and you will become the role model and mentor to aspiring others.

Chapter Seven

The Principle of Accountability

Dr. Bridget–May 2001

The Will to Win

Dr. Bridget–February 2003

THE PRINCIPLE OF ACCOUNTABILITY

Being accountable for your actions helps anchor you in your resolve. Where there is no accountability, there will be a greater opportunity to relapse and get off track. You should become accountable to someone for the goals you set and for the commitment you have made to lose weight and eat healthy. This accountability does not have to be a formal agreement. A simple casual request to a friend or a family member to help you stay on course will often satisfy this component of the discipline developing process.

To provide the professional assistance that I needed in a proper exercise regiment I hired a professional trainer. Hiring the trainer helped in many ways to align us with the principle for accountability. The periodic on sight accountability to the prescribed exercise regiment helped support our will to stick with the program, especially in the early days of the program when we saw very little results.

My children and their spouses, along with my play daughter, divided ourselves into teams. This became fun and caused us to be accountable to others. Daily, we shared the results we were getting and encouraged each other, this strengthened our resolve until we could see the results on the scale and loss of inches.

Dr. Bridget–December 2002

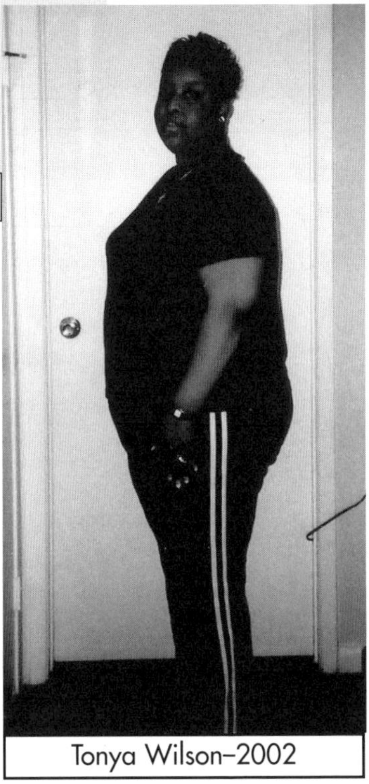

Tonya Wilson–2002

Chapter Eight

The Principle of Saturation

The Will to Win

THE PRINCIPLE OF SATURATION

The Principle of Saturation is quite easy to understand and is somewhat akin to the principle of influence. Saturation by definition is to cause to be filled to completion; to be thoroughly soaked and to reach maximum absorbtion.

Key Statement: Will power, which is the strength of the will to sustain a course of action, is the product of the continuous flow of the information that initially set the will on the desired course.

Our core beliefs which actually govern our decision making and are the anchor points of the will were shaped by four elements. **Core beliefs and values were shaped by:**

1. **Your Environment** - the environment you grew up in has influenced what you believe about life.

2. **Your Authority Figures** - credible other people in your life who taught you, helped establish your beliefs and values.

3. **Repetitious Information** - God has designed us so that what we hear repetitiously impacts and influences our beliefs and values.

4. **Your Life's Experiences** - what you experience in life will most likely be a product of the previously mentioned elements because these establish your expectations. Experiences will normally reinforce the beliefs and values established by the other three components.

Core beliefs were established in our lives when we were very young and impressionable. Whatever belief is established first about a thing becomes a "core belief" and is the basis of decision making and resolve. If the core belief is flawed, the decision making will be flawed and ultimately the resolve will be impaired. The principle of saturation is a method whereby core beliefs that are flawed and that handicap your present pursuit can be uprooted and replaced.

Christians are taught throughout the Bible to do certain things repetitiously so that through the principle of saturation, a transformation can take place. We are taught to meditate in the Word of God day and night in several passages; Psalms 1 and Joshua 1:8.

As you identify flawed core beliefs that hinder your pursuit through the principle of saturation you can over power the erroneous thinking. By repetitiously filling your mind with the information you can in short order establish renewed beliefs which will produce accurate decision making that gives birth to winning behavior.

Now that you know the principles and how they work, the key to working them is a matter of you establishing your will to do so. It is not difficult to learn how to establish your will on a course of beneficial behavior. Let's explore **The Will Setting Process.**

The *Will* to *Win*

CHAPTER NINE

UNDERSTANDING THE WILL-SETTING PROCESS

The *Will* to *Win*

UNDERSTANDING THE WILL-SETTING PROCESS

Before you can take control of the will setting process, you must understand how God engineered the process to work. ***Romans 7:23*** says, ***"But I see another law in my members, warring against the law of my mind,..."*** The law of the mind implies that the mind functions in a certain way all the time. Since God is a God of Order, He has engineered the mental complex of man to function in a consistent manner.

From the observations of scripture and life experiences, there are some outstanding truths that give us insight into how we function mentally. The mind is the center of reasoning where deliberation of the issues of life takes place. This deliberation process has five components that influence its outcome that subsequently impacts the will of man. The will of man carries out the deliberation of the mind by instructing the body to behave based on the information that the mind has processed. This decision process is influenced by five factors that you and I can take control of when we know how to do so.

The five key components of the deliberation process that sets the course of the human will and ultimately controls your life are:

1. The emotional state in which we find ourselves

2. The questions that you choose to ask about the decisions you are about to make

3. The mentor references and accountability factors in your life

4. The pain and pleasure references we make during deliberation

5. The values and beliefs that we have about the issues that are being deliberated

This chapter may be somewhat intimidating to the average Christian who thinks that it is sacrilegious to talk about personally taking control of your life. This is, however, exactly what the Bible teaches that must be done to improve the quality of life.

The great apostle, Paul, wrote to the Christians located in Corinth. In his letter, known as the book of 2nd Corinthians, in the tenth chapter and the fifth verse, Paul tells them to take control of the thoughts that control their lives.

Key Statement: The quality of our lives is conceived by our thoughts, composed by our choices, confirmed by our words and constructed daily by our actions!

The scripture says, ***"Casting down imaginations, and every high thing that exalteth itself against the knowledge of God, and bringing into captivity every thought to the obedience of Christ;" 2 Corinthians 10:3-5***

I was so amazed when I read that it was the will of God for man to be in control of his own will. The Bible is clear on this. In ***1 Corinthians 7:37,*** the apostle Paul states that the man who is control of his own will does well in life.

"Nevertheless he that standeth steadfast in his heart, having no necessity, but hath power over his own will, and hath so decreed in his heart that he will keep his virgin, doeth well." 1 Corinthians 7:37

We must take the conscious initiative to bring this mental process that controls our lives under the authority of the Word of God. To bring the mental process under the authority of the Word of God is to bring our thought process in agreement with what God teaches in the scriptures. As we do things God's way, we will see that His way really works!

Now let's get to work. We want to understand how to cause each of the components of the deliberation process that directs our will to function in a way that will help to transform our behavior God's Way. We will see what the Bible says about each component and then we will show you how to perform it.

Even though our winning pursuit is weight loss and healthy living, the process is generic and can be applied to any endeavor. I want to take you step by step now into next level decision making that I have used for years that has brought me proven success in so many areas of my life. Extracting a practical plan of action from the scriptures is what makes the Bible teaching so relevant and effective. Life becomes exciting when you draft the road map for your future from divine counsel.

Our Emotional State Impacts Our Decisions

Although this is a startling revelation, it is a simple one. The emotions that you experience during deliberation can either negatively or positively impact the outcome of your decision. The Bible teaches us that we are not to be victims of our emotions, but that we should be in control of our emotions while we are making decisions. Jesus says in ***Luke 14:28a, "For which of you, intending to build a tower, sitteth not down first…"*** When it comes to decision-making, Jesus taught the disciples that the person must first sit down, which implies getting control of the emotions surrounding the matter at hand. Again, ***Colossians 3:2*** says, ***"Set your affection on things above, not on things on the earth."*** If we are commanded to set our affection, this means that we have the ability to control the direction of our passion.

Our emotions are neurological triggers that stimulate certain behaviors and feelings. The emotional track will run its course of feelings and behavior unless I purposefully and consciously interrupt the process to give new direction for my emotions. Many people who desire to control their emotions, simply stop and take a deep breath when they sense a negative emotion that will trigger uncomfortable and destructive behavior. This is a simple but effective way of telling your emotions that you are in charge and you will not let this emotion run its course. When I do this repeatedly I will soon retrain my emotions to trigger appropriate behavior.

The Importance of the Questions We Choose to Ask During the Deliberation Process

"For which of you, intending to build a tower, sitteth not down first, and counteth the cost, whether he have sufficient to finish it? Lest haply, after he hath laid the foundation, and is not able to finish it, all that behold it begin to mock him, Saying, this man began to build, and was not able to finish. Or what king, going to make war against another king, sitteth not down first, and consulteth whether he be able with ten thousand to meet him that cometh against him with twenty thousand? Or else, while the other is yet a great way off, he sendeth an ambassage, and desireth conditions of peace." Luke 14:28-32

In this passage, Jesus taught about a military general going to war and choosing to ask certain questions that would keep him on course with his objectives. During deliberation, we are influenced by the questions we choose to ask as we deliberate. Questions we ask provide perspectives. If you have established certain non-negotiable priorities for your life and you purposely make decisions in agreement with those priorities, you will consciously set your will to your desired course.

Establishing priorities requires a little work on your part. Stop now and write ten serious priorities you have for your life. These priorities will serve as your Master Reference Guide for decision-making that will cause you to always choose in agreement with these priorities. The more defined your purpose is, the more impact you will have in the deliberation process. This exercise is very important. You must be honest and take setting these priorities very seriously. Several Master Reference Guides have been provided for you. You should do the following:

1. List in any order on the form the important things and values in your life.

2. Take the time to refine and place in order of importance the items on your list.

3. Take the time to define why these things, relationships, and values are important to you. Be specific and thorough.

4. Review the list and make a copy of it. Keep one copy with you at all times.

Here is a sample list. Refer to the workbook section to complete the exercise.

Priority	Objective	Purpose (Why is this important to you?)
1	God-Obedience and Righteousness	Effective witness, peace and joy within
2	Family-Demonstrate Love	Happiness of family
3	Marriage-Success	Happiness in the home
4	Health-In Excellent Condition	Quality of life
5	Career-Success	Productivity in Life
6	Finance-Wealthy	To support family and the Kingdom of God

When deliberating on a certain issue, I take a deep breath and ask myself the question *"How will this decision impact my decision to please God and obey the principles of righteousness and to serve as a role model for others?"* After I respond to that question, I proceed to the next priority (see #2 in the chart) and question myself on that item as it refers to the nature of the deliberation. I go on and on with questions, making sure that I know how the deliberation interacts with my priorities. These are also pleasurable objectives and can be used in reference to pain and pleasure during decision-making. The priorities should be based on what is most important to you and what you believe to be your life's purpose(s).

The Mentor References and Accountability Factors in Your Life

We are creatures who need acceptance from significant others. The perception of us by our significant others has a great influence on our decision making processes. The two groups of significant others that will impact our decision-making are those whose acceptance we need (friends, support groups, family, etc.) and those who we consider to be our mentors. When we began to make decisions, we subconsciously reference what we believe would be their behavior in a similar situation. Further, we think about how they would feel about our decision.

When we select mentors and others to whom we will be accountable, we must be sure that their values are those that agree with the principles of scripture. These shared values will help to keep our deliberation on a proven course. This is one of the principles by which support groups function. The impact of accountability is sufficient to help those in the support group to hold a course toward beneficial behavior.

The Pain and Pleasure References Made During Deliberation

Key Statement: The will is the gatekeeper of the expressions of the deliberation of the mind.

This is probably one of the most exciting components of the deliberation process. References to pain and pleasure establish the will of man. If you can learn to master this component, you will take charge of the deliberation process and will be able to use it to your advantage. God has designed man to function in a way that makes decision-making quite predictable.

Key Statement: The will is programmed to move away from pain and toward pleasure.

We are designed to move away from pain and toward pleasure! Pain for us denotes possible danger and destruction, so God built within man a system for self preservation. When we sense pain, it becomes an alarm that signals us that the present course is unsafe and must be abandoned. The greater the sense of pain, the greater the threat and the more urgent the flight away from pain. When God presented an important issue to man, He always presented the pros and cons, the good and the bad of things, and the pain and pleasures that would result based on man's decision. These pain and pleasure options impact the decision-making process and causes man to respect this matter and take the deliberative process seriously. A few key verses can easily show the pain and pleasure references that God lays before the decision-maker.

"If ye be willing and obedient, ye shall eat the good of the land: But if ye refuse and rebel, ye shall be devoured with the sword: for the mouth of the LORD hath spoken it." Isaiah 1:19-20

God presents the pain side of a poor decision to encourage man to make the decision toward the pleasure and profitable side.

Again, we can see this in ***Job 36:11-12*** which states, ***"If they obey and serve him, they shall spend their days in prosperity, and their years in pleasures. But if they obey not, they shall perish by the sword, and they shall die without knowledge."***

The power of the pain and pleasure references in decision-making is seen in how people make decisions in their situations. Look at the story of the prodigal son in the fifteenth chapter of Luke. When he sat in the hog pen, he made his decision based on the pain and pleasure reference. While sitting there in the hog pen, he deliberated about his future. He stated that his father had many hired servants with bread enough to spare and he was sitting there perishing with hunger. After this association of pain and pleasure, he decides to move from the pain and toward the pleasure. He said, ***"I will arise and go to my father."***

Key Statement: The will functions in concert with deep-seated beliefs and values until challenged by pain or pleasure.

God has magnificently designed us to make decisions at a conscious and a subconscious level in agreement with the beliefs and values that we have. Decision-making will function in agreement with these values and beliefs until challenged by extreme pain or pleasure.

For example, a morally upright individual would turn down a proposition to get involved in an immoral act until the perceived pleasure of that involvement outweighs the commitment to their values. A single woman, who is morally upright and committed to the values of sexual abstinence before marriage, is approached by a married man to become pregnant and to give birth to a child for him. He offers her $100 to comply with his proposition of having this child. She would immediately turn down the proposition. However, if he raises the stakes and offers her 10 million dollars for her 9-month effort, the perception of the extreme pleasures 10 million dollars could bring to her would cause her to seriously reconsider and even accept the proposition. This proves the point that we all function in concert with deep-rooted beliefs and values until an alternate decision challenges these values with pain or pleasures.

Another revealing illustration of this truth is seen in the dishonest compromises that honest workers are willing to make in the work place when working for dishonest employers. The extreme pain of losing their job outweighs their honest value system. Therefore, they compromise.

Key Statement: When we elevate the pleasurable benefits of a situation above the discomfort or pain caused by the situation, our will is established to endure the short-term discomfort and pain to obtain the pleasurable benefits.

The Bible recorded the intense deliberation of Jesus in the Garden of Gethsemane when He wrestled with the thoughts of dying on the cross. The deliberation was so intense until perspiration, like great drops of blood, ran down his face. Spiritually, Jesus had no problem with doing the Will of the Father. But, at this moment in time, Jesus, the natural man, did not want to die. His flesh rebelled against the idea of dying and His Spirit rejected the idea of experiencing something He had never known: being separated from the Father. Yet, He made the decision to willfully obey the Will of the Father. His deliberation process holds the key to mastering the will in any situation.

The writer of the Book of Hebrews sheds tremendous light on the decision making process of Jesus in the garden. This is the breakthrough principle for establishing the human will in any situation.

"Wherefore seeing we also are compassed about with so great a cloud of witnesses, let us lay aside every weight, and the sin which doth so easily beset us, and let us run with patience the race that is set before us, Looking unto Jesus the author and finisher of our faith; who for the joy that was set before him endured the cross, despising the shame, and is set down at the right hand of the throne of God." Hebrews 12:1-2

You and I can learn to do the same thing that Jesus did to establish His Will. It was difficult for Him, but necessary. ***Hebrews 12:2*** says ***"for the joy that was set***

***before him.*"** This is proof of the previous key statement that says, **When we elevate the pleasurable benefit of a situation above the discomfort or pain caused by the situation, our will is established to endure the short term discomfort and pain to obtain the pleasurable benefit.** Jesus elevated the joy of seeing millions come into the family of God over the ages of time over the pain and discomfort of dying on the cross. We are blessed as a result. His Will enabled Him to make the adjustment to endure the pain for us to gain the benefit.

In our next chapter, I am going to show you how to take this same principle and set your will to overcome poor eating habits, out of control spending habits, procrastination, and even addictions.

The *Will* to *Win*

CHAPTER TEN

ESTABLISHING YOUR WILL

The *Will* to *Win*

ESTABLISHING YOUR WILL

Key Statement: The human will makes small gradual concessions which, when established, forms a new behavior path.

This truth is easily seen in the persuasive approach of the average salesperson. The salesperson attempts to get you to gradually agree with certain undeniable truths about their product. As you progressively agree with one point after another, you find yourself on a course to purchase the product. This truth about how we function gives us the winning advantage when we are choosing to set our will. We understand the magnificent impact of small changes. They soon lead to major transformations.

To bring this process under the control of godliness is quite simple. When pleasing God is established as the major object of my affections and being a righteous example in my generation is my priority, I can now use the aforementioned truth to my advantage.

Key Statement: When pleasing God is the central object of my affections and my Christian witness is of critical importance, any situation, habit or temptation that challenges this commitment is perceived as

emotional pain. As I learn to associate pain with the habits and misbehavior that challenge my commitment to pleasing God and elevate the benefits that accrue from pleasing God, my will can be established to move away from the habit and toward pleasing God.

-.-.-.-.-.-.-.-.-.-.-.-.-.-

Key Statement: Willpower, which is the strength of the will to sustain a course of action, is the product of the continuous flow of the information that initially set the will on the desired course.

-.-.-.-.-.-.-.-.-.-.-.-.-.-

Key Statement: Pain Reference Enhancers help magnify the impact of undesirable habits and behavior to enforce the establishment of the will on a more desirable course.

-.-.-.-.-.-.-.-.-.-.-.-.-.-

The stronger the pain reference, the greater the impact is on the will setting systems. We can deliberately magnify the pain of a continuous undesirable behavior through pain reference enhancers. This will assist the will setting process. An enhancer is a visual or an audible element or a combination of both that can be used to make the undesirable behavior or outcome repulsive. Vivid photographs or video documentaries can be used.

Quick Application: This principle is so simple yet so powerful. I want to jump start you with the pain and pleasure reference to help you lose weight. You must associate pain with your present obese overweight state! To help you intensify that pain you should spend some time thinking about people who have suffered a lesser quality of life because of their overweight state. Think of dying and not being able to spend the quality time with your family. Dying and not being able to live a productive life of service to God. Locate pictures that will help imprint the message of pain, by looking in magazines for truly obese people. I have advised some who don't like shot needles to go purchase a few shot needles and look at it knowing that to continue is to risk possible diabetes, which could mean being chained to a needle for the rest of your life. As you saturate you mind with these pain references, your will is being stimulated to move you toward a behavior that will not bring on the pain!

We are now ready to move to the final and most exciting part of this presentation, which is the practical application of the principles we have covered in this teaching. In our final session, we will review the relative principles and demonstrate step by step how to use these principles in transforming undesirable behavior.

The *Will* to *Win*

CHAPTER ELEVEN

PRACTICAL APPLICATION OF THE WILLPOWER PRINCIPLES

The *Will* to *Win*

PRACTICAL APPLICATION OF THE WILLPOWER PRINCIPLES

Winning in the situations of life is a matter of the will. You may hear the sportscasters saying prior to a sports contest with equally talented and matched teams that the outcome will be determined by the team with the will to win. Weight loss and fat loss programs, by and large, all work. The determining factor in losing weight, provided there are no medical problems, is the will to follow the plan.

We have covered a great deal of information on behavioral change and now it's time to put together the nuts and bolts of a plan of action that you can follow to effect change in your life. To apply any truth or principle, in this case a spiritual principle, there are four things that are required. First, you need a revelation of the principle, which is an understanding of the principle at the level of your comprehension. Secondly, you need a role model; you need to see the principle lived out in the lives of others. Thirdly, you need a regiment of faith, which is a systematic way to apply the principle that has yielded results for others and will yield results for you. Finally, you need a righteous resolve; this is a positive, beneficial, righteous reason for the success of this principle.

Developing and working your strategy requires following a simple step-by-step plan of action repetitiously until you get the desired results. It's like the assembly of toys at Christmas. You must do four things to successfully assemble the toys. You will need a picture of the end results, confidence in the assembly instructions, proper tools that are required for assembly, and you will need to follow the instructions in a correct and systematic order.

Review of Principles

You and I must develop a life-change program that will put us on course and keep us on course with goals and purposes for our lives. The components of your personal plan will be the application of several principles we have already talked about. Let's review several of them.

> **The Principle of Faith Confession** - What you say impacts your life. Based on the power of words as taught in the scriptures, you will be instructed to say something on a regular basis that will have tremendous impact on your behavior.

The Principle of Dominant Influence - Your environment. You must evaluate those around you to determine who will support your effort to change and those who will ridicule your effort to change. You may need to redefine certain relationships in order to develop a workable plan.

The Principle of Accountability - Having someone to monitor your commitment. This principle is based on our need for acceptance, which causes us to make necessary adjustments when we must report our actions to others.

The Principle of Saturation - Absorbing information on the new direction you want to take in life. This principle is the foundation for changing negative beliefs that prohibit consistent winning behavior. Reading this book and other books on those who lost weight and gained control of eating is good saturation material.

Review of Factors About the Will

- The will is the gatekeeper for the expression of the mind.

- The will is programmed to move away from pain and to move toward pleasure.

- The will functions in concert with deep-seated beliefs and values until challenged by pain or pleasure.

- When we elevate the pleasurable benefits of a situation above the discomfort or pain caused by the situation, our will is established to endure the short-term discomfort and pain to obtain the pleasurable benefits.

- The human will makes small, gradual concessions, which when established, forms a new behavior path.

- When pleasing God is the central object of my affections and my Christian witness is of critical importance, any situation, habit or temptation that challenges this commitment is perceived as emotional pain. As I learn to associate pain with the habits and misbehavior that challenge my commitment to pleasing God and elevate the benefits of pleasing God, my will can be established to move away from the habit and toward pleasing God.

- Willpower, which is the strength of the will to sustain a course of action, is the product of the continuous flow of the information that initially sets the will on the desired course. A break in the flow of information is the cause for relapse and failure.

- The will makes small concessions that are monumental in their importance to transformation.

The *Will* to *Win*

CHAPTER TWELVE

THE SEVEN STEPS TO WILLPOWER DEVELOPMENT

The *Will* to *Win*

THE SEVEN STEPS TO WILLPOWER DEVELOPMENT

Now that we have reviewed, we are ready for our seven application steps to willpower development.

Step One

Complete the Life's Priorities Form.

Step Two

Identify the habit you need to break or change.

Step Three

Repeat *"I Can do all things through the power of God which strengthens me"* ten times.

Step Four

Ask yourself these probing questions aloud and take time to write the answers. Use the **Pain Reference Form** that is provided.

1. How does negative habits negatively effect:
    - My relationship with God?
    - My relationship with my family?

- My career?
- My health?

2. What profit will breaking this habit afford me?

   - How will my life be better? (write it down)

3. Who do I know that has overcome a similar problem or habit? *If possible, call them up.*

4. Who can support me in my effort to change?

   - Get the phone numbers of these significant others, call them, and ask for their help and encouragement.

Step Five
Locate Pain Reference Enhancers. Find photos and/or books that will help you magnify the pain of staying on your present course of action. The more devastating the enhancer the more effective the impact will be.

Step Six
Develop your personal pain and pleasure affirmation on a regular basis. This is an exciting step.

Samples of Pain and Pleasure References

Pain References

How will this affect my…	SMOKING CIGARETTES
Relationship with God?	My witness will not be credible. I will not be able to effectively fulfill my purpose.
Relationship with Spouse?	My spouse will have to care for me because of health challenges. My spouse will probably be widowed. Another person will help him/her spend my insurance money. I will be unattractive to my spouse: yellow teeth, bad breath, stinky clothes and hair.
Relationship with Children?	My children will become smokers because I am modeling that behavior for them. My children may become sick from the second hand smoke.
Health?	My health will be challenged: cancer, respiratory problems, poor blood circulation, heart disease, and lung disease. I will die an early death.
Finances and Career	Buying cigarettes is a waste of money. I will have to take days off because of health challenges. I will have to spend money on higher insurance and hospital bills.

Pleasure References

How will this affect my...	NOT SMOKING CIGARETTES
Relationship with God?	My witness will be credible. I will be able to effectively fulfill my purpose.
Relationship with Spouse?	My spouse will not have to care for me because of health challenges caused by smoking. My spouse and I will be able to enjoy each other.
Relationship with Children?	My children will not have smoking modeled for them by the most significant other in their lives. I provide a healthy environment for my children.
Health?	My health will not be challenged due to smoking
Finances and Career	The money I would have used to by cigarettes, to pay for higher insurance, doctor bills, and hospital visits may be used for something more productive. My health will not be a factor in the success of my career.

Associate enough pain until you make the shift in the way you think about cigarettes. The shift will happen. Although the shift may not be dramatic at first, remember that every little concession is a monumental step toward success!

Step Seven

Call a friend and let them know what you have done. Make yourself accountable and hold your course. You are developing the will to win!

When you begin to do these seven steps repetitiously, you will experience results.

I have prepared a section in the appendix to help in your retention of this information. I drafted certain questions, along with an answer key, to allow you to test yourself on these life-changing principles. I trust that you understand what is at stake here. A new quality of life can be yours if you put forth the effort to learn these principles. You may use the sample pain and pleasure references to assist you or you may develop your own. The more graphic and impactful the better. The next chapter will deal with the weight loss regiment my family and I used to get the results of which we are so proud. After this next chapter, you will be on your way to a better place in life because you will have the tools and the knowledge to change!

The *Will* to *Win*

CHAPTER THIRTEEN

THE REGIMENTATION

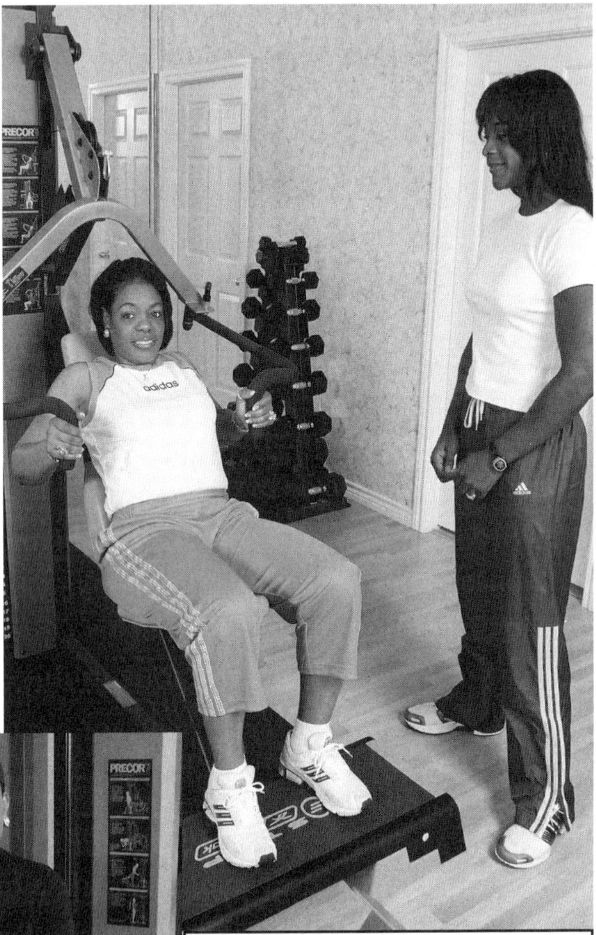

Dr. Bridget and Victoria "Jazz"
doing exercise regiment
June 2003

Tonya Wilson–June 2003

THE REGIMENTATION

This chapter of the book deals with the actual development and implementation of a winning strategy. As I mentioned before discipline and focus was not a weakness in my pursuit of any of the weight loss plans I tried, although they worked for others, none of them yielded the results I was looking for. If you have difficulty staying on course with plans and programs, I suggest that you review the previous chapter and go step-by-step through the process outlined to establish a life-changing resolve to lose weight.

My winning regiment was twofold: it involved a nutritional plan and an exercise program. In this chapter I will share insights into both plans. Remember, this book is not intended to serve as medical counsel to you or to serve as a consultation from a professional on weight management. Investing in the professional help you need, will be money well spent. Reading books by professionals will also serve as an asset as you acquire the knowledge you need for the journey. As I step you through the winning strategy my trainer and nutritionist developed for me, I trust that you will be inspired to take affirmative action today to make corrections in your health and weight loss pursuits.

The scripture testifies of the importance of a work effort in order to make gains. The writer of the book of James documented an incredible revelation that really puts things in perspective. ***James*** says in chapter ***3*** verse ***17,*** "Even so faith, if it hath not works, is dead, being alone." There must be sufficient corresponding action according to a well thought out plan of action drafted by someone with proven results. Developing a workable plan of action that flows with your lifestyle is critical to your success.

The Exercise Regiment

On January 20, 2003, I had my first training session with Victoria. Victoria, a member of our church and a professional weight trainer, was equally excited about our pursuit for weight loss and health. Victoria, who we call "Jazz" (nickname from her former days as a professional Gladiator), came highly recommended. I knew of several other ladies whom she had worked with, and their results were astounding.

However, after working with Jazz about two weeks, I became a little concerned because I expected fast and immediate results from the intense workouts. I was disappointed that I had only lost a few pounds; nothing to brag about. Prior to the having a trainer, my weight had skyrocketed to 215 pounds. This was my weight on

January 1, 2003, which spurred me to start my "no eating after 7:00 p.m." crash plan. This was just another one of my many diet plans I have tried over the years. Not eating after 7:00 p.m. was no problem for me. Anything I set my mind to do, I have developed the willpower to do it. This crash plan resulted in a 5 pound weight loss. My disappointment however, was that after working out like a "Trojan" with a trainer after six days (January 26, 2003), I still weighed 210 pounds.

Jazz initially suggested that I visit a nutritionist, but the next available appointment was February 7, 2003. So, I continued with the trainer three days a week–Monday, Wednesday and Friday–and worked out without a trainer the other days of the week. She designed a daily cardio routine (exercise designed to strengthen your heart and body), which I followed to the letter.

The morning and evening exercise regiment was progressive and involved a variety of physical calisthenics, cardio routine (treadmill or step machine) and stretching routines. I started with about 20 minutes of cardio, then after two weeks it was increased to 30 minutes, then to 45 minutes and after three months 60 minutes of cardio exercise. On Tuesdays and Thursdays, I used the same cardio routine, only without the trainer. I could have rested one day, however, I would do the exercise regiment only once a day on Saturdays and Sundays.

On February 7, 2003, when I walked into the nutritionist's office, I weighed a whopping 207 pounds. I was amazed as she began to take my measurements. I have a chart to show my progress on another page. Although Margo's (the nutritionist) scale seemed to be about 6 pounds above my scale at home, I was still a bit embarrassed and shocked. I had heard that you always weigh more after eating breakfast and my appointment was after breakfast, but this was ridiculous.

I had my last visit with Margo on June 16, 2003, and all of my measurements and weight had improved so drastically. I have a new appreciation for gaining the expertise in both exercise and eating to get significant results. On June 16, 2003, I weighed in at 174 pounds according to Margo's scale, which is about 6 pounds above my home scale, which showed 168 pounds that morning prior to breakfast. At any rate, that's a 33 to 39 pound weight loss in only 4 months, and when I share the cholesterol report, you will be astounded even more. Based on my weight of 215 pounds in January of 2003, I have experienced a 41 to 47 pound weight loss. Now that's pretty impressive if I say so myself!

The initial investment in the nutritionist proved to be a quality investment that provides the professional expertise I needed to develop a winning health strategy. I was so enlightened on that first visit. I immediately knew all the things I had done wrong in the past that were counter-productive to my weight reduction goals. I found out that the crash diets, the starvation plans and the yo-yo diets had done more harm than good to my metabolism.

The Eating Regiment

Margo instructed me to eat six meals per day instead of my one meal midday and starving until the next day. Yes, that's right; **six meals!** Later in the book, I will share some sample meals with you. The purpose of the six meal a day plan was to keep my metabolism going. The nutritionist explained that the work of the metabolism is to burn fat. When you eat breakfastt that initiates the fire and starts the process, just when the flame is about to die down (2-3 hours later), you have to add more fuel (food) to the fire.

The goal the nutritionist established for me was to keep all fat intake below 20% of a particular food source. Much to my amazement, the labels on most foods are very misleading. As I sat in her office, she pulled out package labels and showed me how to read fat percentage in foods. The formula is quite simple. It's the calories from fat divided by total calories which equals percentage of fat. For example, a package of luncheon meat that says it has 20 calories per serving and 7 calories from fat per serving, along with the advertiser boasting 97% fat free sounds great if that information is really correct. Based on the formula, 7 calories divided by 20 is 35% fat. So that means this would be over the 20% fat intake from a food source, which means to obtain my goal, I had to leave that luncheon meat in the grocery store.

I know you are probably saying, like I did, *"lunch meat can't be that bad,"* but I was amazed. Try it. Take your calculator to the grocery store when you shop, or look in your refrigerator right now. As of this date, I have not found any luncheon meat, not even turkey luncheon meat, that falls in the 20% goal range.

The first visit, as you can see, was quite a learning experience. I became a calculator shopping queen as I adapted my lifestyle to the new plan. I also began to keep a daily journal of my food and water intake. I had to eliminate all oils and butters, so hot sauce, picante sauce, butter sprays and other seasonings began to have a delightful taste.

Now, let's talk about what I did eat.

Breakfast

- 4 egg whites scrambled–no butter, no oil.

  There are wonderful cooking sprays on the market that can be used to scramble eggs. To add some excitement to my eggs, I added vegetables like bell peppers, green onions and tomatoes

- 1 serving of Carbohydrates (see full list below), such as oatmeal, rice, potatoes, or grits–no butter, no oil.

  Note: Only one serving of either of the above carbohydrates, not one serving of each. ☺

  On mornings when I was in a rush, I would have a whole-wheat breakfast wrap. This consists of a whole-wheat tortilla, egg whites, and a little brown rice. I found a health food store that had them already packaged. All I had to do was pop them in the microwave for 2-3 minutes and I was off to another exciting day.

  Note: These wraps cannot be purchased from a regular grocery store. There is a health food store in the Houston area that works along with the nutritionist to make sure the quantity size and serving size are proper. I don't know if they ship around the world but if you write me I will gladly give you the name of the company.

Mid-Morning snack (2-3 hours after Breakfast)

- 1 piece of fruit or non-fat yogurt

  Note: Check your labels and do the formula because some are tricky. You can make your yogurt more exciting by adding oats.

Lunch (2-3 hours after Mid-Morning Snack)

- 4-5 oz. of lean meat, such as Chicken or Fish,–no butter no oil

  The serving size of the meat may vary for each person. The pattern is that the meat portion should be the size of your hand, spread out with fingers touching.

- 1 starch (the size of a fist)–no butter no oil

  The following are starches or carbohydrates and serving sizes that can be eaten during lunch and breakfast:

Barley	1 cup
Beans	1 cup
Black-eyed Peas	1 cup
Bread (40-45 calories per slice)	2 slices
Corn	1 cup
Corn Tortillas	2
Cream of Wheat, Rice, or Rye (see pckg. for 1 serving size)	1 serving
Kashi	1 cup
Lentils	1 cup
Oatmeal	1 cup
Pasta (only once per week)	1 cup
Peas	1 cup
Potato	8 oz
Yam (sweet potato)	8 oz
Rice	1 cup
Rice Cakes	5

Remember, no butter and no oil
during preparation or eating.

The following vegetables are on the "no limit" list, which means that there is no limit to the amount you can eat and retain a healthy diet.

Artichoke	Celery	Radishes
Asparagus	Eggplant	Shallots
Bamboo Shoots	Green Beans	Spinach
Broccoli	Leeks	Spaghetti Squash
Brussels	Lettuce	Sprouts
Sprouts	Mushrooms	Tomato
Cabbage	Okra	Water Chestnuts
Carrots	Onions	Zucchini
Cauliflower	Peppers	

Remember, no butter and no oil
during preparation or eating.

If you choose to have a salad, remember the formula. Most salad dressings are loaded with oil. The best rule for eating salads is with plain or balsamic vinegar and fresh lemon juice. If you must have salad dressing, try dipping your fork in the dressing and then touch your salad and enjoy. Never just pour the salad dressing onto salad because it adds way too much fat to your meal.

Mid-Afternoon Snack (2-3 hours after Lunch)

■ 1 piece of fruit or air-popped popcorn–no butter, no oil

Dinner (2-3 hours after Mid Afternoon Snack)

■ 4-5 oz. lean meat–no butter, no oil

■ Vegetables from the above list–no butter, no oil

Note: No starch for dinner and no carbohydrates after 6:00 p.m.

Evening Snack (2-3 hours after Dinner)

■ 4-5 oz. protein with vegetables–no butter, no oil

Make sure your evening snack is at least 2-3 hours before retiring for the evening. It is not a good idea to go to bed with a full stomach.

I usually save some of my protein (meat portion) from dinner, if the serving was more than I needed, and eat that as my evening snack. It is alright to skip the evening snack if you are retiring early.

Important: Drink one-half your body weight in ounces of water per day. For example, my daily intake of water is 90 ounces. Diet sodas and tea are alright with no sugar in the tea. I use an artificial sweetener and only two diet sodas a day. To substitute for oil and butter, I use a butter spray. Make sure it is a spray because the tubs and the sticks don't qualify for the formula.

I also use a lot of sauces like picante, hot sauce, low calorie salsa, and if you like sour cream, fat free sour cream is alright.

Please note that you should consult your physician or nutritionist before starting any plan. I am not a physician nor a nutritionist.

I will share my progress with you on each of my visits to the nutritionist. She took my measurements and the results are listed below.

MEASURE	DATE	DATE	DATE	DATE	DATE	DATE
	2/7/03	2/24/03	3/14/03	4/18/03	5/19/03	6/16/03
Tricep	92	44	40	35	31	28
Bicep	16	15	15	11	10	9
Subscap.	51	40	35	31	30	26
Supra.	30	30	28	28	22	18
Pec	20	16	14	12	8	8
Ab	52	49	45	31	26	24
Kidney	52	47	37	37	29	29
Quad	46	41	39	34	30	28
Calve	18	18	18	18	15	15
% Fat	43.74%	40.23%	37.93%	34.56%	30.24%	28.62%
Fat Pounds ↓	90.76	81.26	72.71	63.76	54.13	50.01
Lean Bodymass	116.74	120.74	121.04	120.74	124.87	124.74

It was so refreshing to visit with the nutritionist on 6/16/03 and graduate to the maintenance program. It has been challenging but fun to go from a size 16 in my favorite designer to now size 6 and 8. In other designers I am in a 10 but that is fine with me. I will probably lose a few more pounds, but the joy of knowing with discipline and self control I can maintain this healthy life for another seventy three years or so.

Insight from Victoria, the Personal Trainer

When Dr. Bridget first approached me about being her weight trainer I thought, *"what a blessing!"* This occurred when I was about to make some major changes in my career. I was strongly considering going into real estate with my husband full-time and either reducing the weight training career to a minimum or basically eliminating it all together.

I love weight training and I take it very seriously. It is a great joy to train someone like Dr. Bridget because she is strongly committed to the Word of God and to a lifestyle of fitness.

The first thing I considered in training Dr. Bridget was her body type. Then I developed a program for her that would be productive. As you know, several members of her family joined in on the program, so everyone was divided into body types and goals. Once that was established, it was easy to work with them. However, my focus for this section is Dr. Bridget, so allow me to discuss the general conditions and reasoning for her and her team.

General Conditioning/Reason and Team

Your Personal Training Program should always be designed to aid you in developing your goals and support your reasons for starting your journey to improved health. You always want to check with your physician to qualify your plans for what will be a demanding process.

Next, determine your reason for the change for improved health. Develop your ***WHY.*** This is a method used in many areas of life. Your reason sets the foundation for your purpose. The Word of God says, ***"Therefore whosoever heareth these sayings of mine, and doeth them, I will liken him unto a wise man, which built his house upon a rock: 25 And the rain descended, and the floods came, and the winds blew, and beat upon that house; and it fell not: for it was founded upon a rock. 26 And every one that heareth these sayings of mine, and doeth them not, shall be likened unto a foolish***

man, which built his house upon the sand." Matthew 7:24-26. Simply stated, you should build on a solid foundation that will stand. It is wise to include a team of individuals to help in carrying out your plan. This team can consist of supportive family members, nutritionists, physicians, supportive friends and any other positive tool you can rely on.

The Process

This process is tailored to Dr. Bridget's body type and goals. Everyone has a different body type and goal therefore, this may or may not work for you. I strongly recommend that after reading Dr. Bridget's program, you seek the wisdom of your physician and nutritionist. Together you can obtain a program that is suited for you.

Be advised that Dr. Bridget's program is not easy and it is not for everyone. Together we took the most aggressive approach to weight loss used by many professional athletes. She is a strong woman and can accomplish anything she puts her mind and will to. I knew that I was working with a person of principle and felt that I could "push the envelope" on giving her a strenuous program. She would be closely monitored and the necessary changes would be made along the way.

Okay, on to the point of training . . . THE PROCESS. I suggest you educate yourself on the different body types and determine whether you are a beginner, an intermediate or an advanced. In my opinion there are three body types–an endomorph, ectomorph and mesomorph. You will most likely fall into one of these categories.

Decide on where you are and where you want to be. Make certain your goals are reasonable. Personally, I recognized that I am a large boned individual and therefore my goal of visiting the petite section will forever be out of the question. Start by having a long-term goal with short-team goals along the way.

Develop a program that you can maintain for 3-4 weeks. Keep in mind that during this time there will be other influences that could cause you to alter, but hold your course.

Do not be influenced by your scale. Muscle weighs more than fat, and it is not uncommon to gain before you lose.

I suggest you find a good gym that allows you to have variations. I use a variety of programs to help my clients obtain their goals. When you're considering hiring of a trainer, always select a trainer with proven success and several references.

Dr. Bridget's Workout Equipment

■A Universal with 3 Stacks:

■ Weights with Leg Extensions, Leg Curl, Bench Press, Incline Press, Decline Press, Front Pull Downs, Biceps Curls, Triceps Press Downs, Abdominal, Butterflies

■ 2 Lifecycle Treadmills

■ Elliptical: Cardio equipment

■ Accessories include: Close Grip Bars, Pronated Grip Bars, Rope, Single-hand Grips, Wide Grip Bars

■ Dumbbells: 3 lbs – 20 lbs

■ Balls: Resist Exercise and Medicine

■ Ankle Weights

■ 40 lb Body Vest

■ Floor Mats: for floor exercises

Dr. Bridget's Planned Process

Dr. Bridget's and her family's process consisted of circuit training during the first month. This was designed to condition the individual at their level of performance.

I ran this program in conjunction with the results of the nutritionist. I always monitored the muscle to fat ratio. I try not to make changes based on watching the scale, which will cause you to second guess your program. Trusting your trainer is critical.

Dr. Bridget's cardio program started with 20 minutes twice a day with intervals on the Precore. The intensity was governed by her target heart rate. When you perform within your target heart rate, your time becomes more constructive. Within a two week period, Dr. Bridget showed no progress as far as her weight, but I knew her ratio was changing. Her second visit to the nutritionist proved to be correct. I then increased her cardio to 20 minutes in the morning and 30-40 minutes at night and considered moving her to the treadmill for variety. You will find that the body will acclimate very quickly to it's conditions, therefore it helps if you have a trainer who can see these changes come about and make the necessary moves to keep the system moving.

My next phase was to listen to what was being said. Comments often tell you which direction will be more productive. I then decided to have everyone record their eating habits. This process helps everyone to see if they really have control of the eating. This step proved to be very productive. At certain levels of your training, the body should respond in certain ways. As a trainer, I monitor this process very closely.

Between the third and fourth month, I increased the intensity of cardio with running by intervals–run a minute, walk a minute. Dr. Bridget's program, along with everyone else's, is changed based upon and designed around monthly results and measurements. Everyone in the family now trains chest, triceps-shoulders, legs, back and biceps. I have her to do abs every time we meet. I think you can do abs as long as you do not include weights on every session. However, I keep an open mind to change in the midst of the training session if I see that it is necessary. The cardio is now increased to 45 minutes in the morning and 45 minutes at night on Tuesdays, Thursdays, once on Saturdays or Sundays, 45 minutes. On Mondays, Wednesdays, and Fridays, cardio for 45 minutes at night. Please keep in mind that I make this decision based on the body types of each person.

Dispelling the Myths

Here are some of many myths to weight training or even attempting weight train.

1. *I'll get bigger if I lift weights.*

   Someone once gave me the best comment on describing this myth. *"Weights do not have calories."* Lifting is designed to aid in shaping and toning the body. Your diet determines your size. You cannot eat a Thanksgiving dinner at each meal and expect to maintain a lean toned body.

2. *My whole family looks like this, so I guess I will too.*

   Wrong! You can break that curse. Grant it, certain cultures have their trademark, but I do not have to have a full backside just because my mom had one. Change that record!

3. *I do 500 sit-ups daily and this stomach will not go away, so, that's the way it is.*

   Wrong again! That plan needs modification. Usually the person performs that exercise too fast, without detail and proper form. I do not do 500 sit-ups or crunches and I still gain the results I need and desire. This area, along with the lower extremities, seems to take longer. I believe wherever you gained first will come off last. Be patient.

amazon.com

Billing Address:
Claudia Beamus
4823 VALLA RD
LOUISVILLE, KY 40213-2941
United States

SDtZCG1ndR

Shipping Address:
Claudia Beamus
4823 VALLA RD
LOUISVILLE, KY 40213-2941
United States

Returns Are Easy!
Visit http://www.amazon.com/returns to return any item - including gifts - in unopened or original condition within 30 days for a full refund (other restrictions apply)

Your order of September 25, 2008 (Order ID:002 -- 1367880 -- 2489056)

Qty	Item	Item Price	Total
	IN THIS SHIPMENT		
3	**Redemption** (** P-4-B51G3 **) 5000X1L64U 5000X1L64U 5000X1L64U **Hardcover**	$4.99	$14.97

Subtotal	$14.97
Shipping & Handling	$5.97
Tax	$1.26
Order Total	$22.20
Paid via Mastercard	$22.20
Balance Due	$0.00

This shipment completes your order.

8945 (3 of 3)

SDtZCG1ndR

amazon.com and you're done.

30/DtZCG1ndR/-3 of 3-//CP/std-4-us/4156380/0927-00:30/0925-15:17/sp091738945/1-1 Z1

4. *It takes too many hours in the day to train, so I cannot entertain the thought of training.*

   It depends on what you're looking for. If you can revamp your time in the day, you would be surprised at how you can incorporate it into your daily routine. For example, if you have an hour for lunch, you can get in 30 minutes of cardio and still have time for lunch. Plan ahead. Bring your food with you (which you should do any way if you have set a plan to lose weight). When lunch-time arrives, start your cardio, then spend 15 minutes eating and the rest pulling yourself together to return to work. I know this works because I have done this for over 15 years. If you have the will, you can make the way. The question is, do you have the will?

Dr. Bridget–June 2003

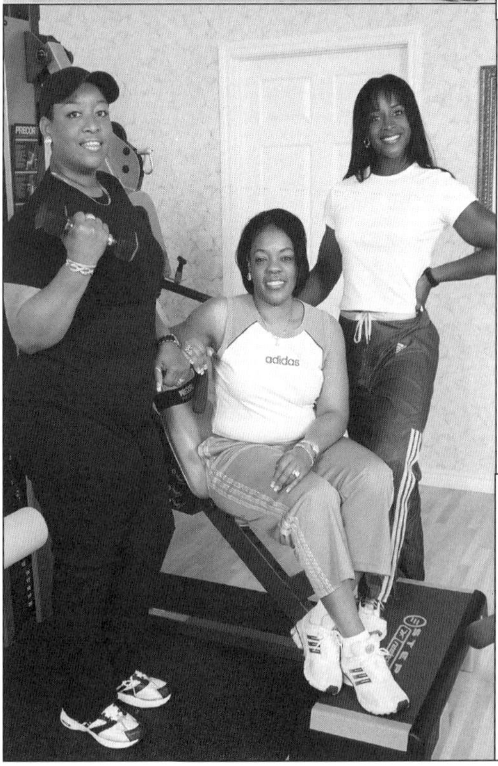

Left to Right:
Tonya Wilson
(Dr. Bridget's workout partner);
Dr. Bridget;
Victoria "Jazz" Gay-Moore,
Personal Trainer

CHAPTER FOURTEEN

THE REWARDS

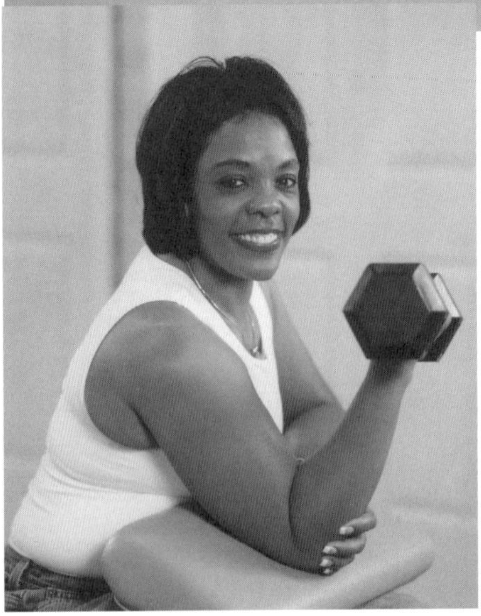

Dr. Bridget–July 2003

THE REWARDS

Since winning is obtaining some predetermined goal, the rewards of the process must be meaningful, otherwise it is difficult to make a demand on the effort required for winning. Keeping your eye on the prize is stimulating if the prize is of value.

In recapping my journey after obtaining the prize, loss of weight, healthy lifestyle and great doctor's report, let it be known that I am enjoying the prize. Let me close this final chapter with encouragement to you to develop the will power resolve to reach your goal. A major element of the process is the self imposed restraints you are willing to place on your life to stay the course. So many people have lofty goals and dreams who have embarked on many a noteworthy journey only to yield to the first obstacle, difficulty or temptation. The strength of your resolve is measured by the restraints you are willing to impose to stay on course with the winning objective.

Choosing to Possess Your Vessel

"That every one of you should know how to possess his vessel in sanctification and honour."1 Thessalonians 4:4

Resisting temptation to yield to weaknesses is the mark of focused resolve. Unless you are honest with yourself about those things that will derail your purpose you will not be fortified against their pull. For me, there are two food passions that I have that are detrimental to my health and new lifestyle regiment: chocolate candy, and peanut butter. I choose to reach my goals therefore I made a decision not to eat these snacks, but replaced them with snacks that are more beneficial to me. I have associated more pain with those foods that are harmful to me and a greater sense of pleasure to those foods that are beneficial to me, thus my will is established to steer me away from painful things toward the pleasurable.

One of the first things the nutritionist asked was how many times do you eat out? I told her that about 90% of my eating is in restaurants. My husband and I have a very extensive travel schedule, ministering in churches across America which causes us to eat in many restaurants. The nutritionist informed me that it would probably be more difficult for me because I traveled so much. You know what? She was right! However, I refused to use this as an excuse to compromise both my eating program or exercise program. I had to literally train people to prepare my food. In ordering my food, either through room service or at a restaurant, I had to get quite specific. I had to say things like *"no oil and no butter in preparing my food please."* In many cases, I had to just order boiled eggs and eat the white only. There were times when if I could not watch the people prepare my food, they would scramble my eggs with oil or butter and when the food got to me, it would be all greasy and buttery. On those occasions, I would politely have them prepare the food the way I ordered it.

This is the discipline and determination you have when you associate enough pain with the distasteful alternatives to your winning strategy. It really is not that difficult. You see, I began to equate oil and butter to the high cholesterol which leads to heart disease and possibly a lifestyle of taking medicines with severe side effects attached to them. NO, this was not the way for me! Again, I remind you, I moved away from pain and towards pleasure. These principles were explained in detail in chapter two. I recommend that you go back and review them, do the exercise and break free of destructive behavior.

My nutritionist told me that in order to get the desired results, I would have to give up fried foods. Like most people, I love fried fish, chicken and shrimp, but to accomplish my goal, I equated pain with those foods so that I could establish my will to resist the temptation. I readily made the decision to change to grilled meats, such as chicken, fish, and shrimp. Can you imagine eating a baked potato without butter? Well, I do. Instead of butter, I use a substitute for butter–a butter spray. I know this may all sound distasteful, but when you associate the pain of needle injections, and possible blindness due to diabetes from being overweight, the decision is not difficult.

My eating regiment allows me to have 40 grams of sugar a day, which means occasionally, I do eat something sweet. I have proven that I am a disciplined person and can handle that. When I say I am going to do something, because I have developed the will to win in a situation, I can do exactly what I need to do.

I know that you are probably thinking, *"Have you ever slipped and eaten any of the foods that were not on your program?"* The answer to that is initially NO. I am very disciplined and focused on what I eat and the plan is not as rigid as it may sound. I am able to make certain adjustments to splurge within moderation occasionally. Any moderation is quickly followed by a more intense exercise regiment and eating discipline. It's a lifestyle not a diet!

This lifestyle is a commitment to overcome every obstacle to stay on track and never hide behind an excuse to fail to follow the winning strategy. It would amaze you what I have had to overcome just to use hotel exercise facilities when my husband and I are in ministry in other cities. My evening exercise normally takes place before I retire for the evening which would be after we return from an evening worship service. Most hotels use late nights to clean their exercise facilities or simply close them during late evening hours. My secretary checks beforehand when making our travel arrangements to ensure that I will have access to the exercise facilities after church services. Where there is a will, there is always a way!

I am now enjoying the rewards of months of very hard work and maintaining is half as difficult as it was attaining. I lost the desired weight of 45 pounds and I have maintained my present weight. I am in the desired size 8 dress in my favorite designer collection. The photos testify of what discipline and a constructive work effort can produce. My husband tells me that I look great! I feel great and my physical stamina is evident in every thing I do, from ministry of the word to long walks in the shopping mall (smile). I am thankful to God for this incredible plan of action that has yielded the results that I was praying for.

On June 16, 2003, my doctor checked my blood work and the news is great! January 2003's high cholesterol count of 179 has fallen to an incredible 146 LDB without any medication; just discipline, hard work and the willpower to win.

As stated in an earlier chapter, every plan will work if you discipline yourself and set your will to work it. Find the plan that works for you. Stop making excuses! You say you are busy, so am I, I continue to assist my husband in ministry and we travel two to three weeks each month. As I stated earlier, I eat at restaurants about 90% of the time and I have accomplished my goal. It is especially important to know that between the visits to the nutritionist on May 19, 2003 and June 16, 2003 I continued to exercise, but not with the trainer because I was traveling. You MUST abandon all excuses. You can achieve your goals. Keep the Will to Win!

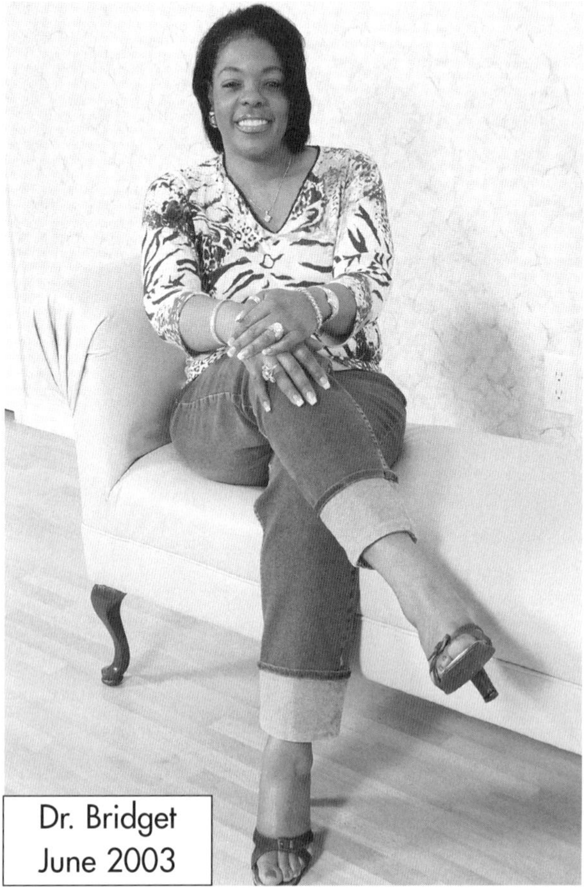

Dr. Bridget
June 2003

APPENDIX

The *Will* to *Win*

FAQs

Dr. Bridget E. Hilliard

1. **How did you lose weight?** I hired a weight trainer and a nutritionist. Together we worked on my weight loss program that has become a lifestyle.

2. **Why did you lose weight?** I had to lower my cholesterol without medication, and on the vanity side I had a desire to look better in my clothes.

3. **What kept you motivated on the program?** I had a dress size 12 and a picture of the way I looked years ago and this kept me motivated.

4. **Why did you choose Victoria "Jazz?"** I chose "Jazz" because I saw the results in her own life and the lives of other women in the church she had trained.

5. **Would you recommend to someone to do the same thing you did?** Yes, just not as aggressive as I did because it was challenging at times, but I got the results that I wanted plus I strongly recommend that you go to your Physician first like I did, get a thorough exam and be willing to trust the people that

God will raise up in your life to help you on your course to weight loss.

6. **Why did you choose to be a size 10 and not a smaller size, I thought thin means healthy?** Actually this is not the case; never confuse a smaller size with better health because this is not always true. I have read many books that back me up on this and I suggest you get some reference material to help educate yourself on this misconception. I chose a size 10 because I didn't want to look sick or have a really small body and a big head. Although I am now a size 8 in my favorite designer and a 10 in other designers I am happy with the results. It appears they make prettier things in 8 and 10.

Victoria "Jazz" Gay-Moore

1. **Will Dr. Bridget's program work for me?** Well, yes and no. Some of the things that Dr. Bridget did may work for you and you may get results but for the most part you need to contact your physician, a personal trainer and a nutritionist who can design a program just for you.

2. **How much do you cost, you must be expensive?** My rates are not too low and not too high.

3. **How do I get rid of the side roll and the flabby**

arms? I recommend diet and exercise to eliminate the two, but again seek your physician, a weight trainer and a nutritionist.

4. **What did you do when Dr. Bridget did not see the results she was looking for in the first few weeks of the program?** I have seen this before and I have to tell you I was not moved by that at all. In fact, I recommended to her after 2-3 weeks to go see a nutritionist.

5. **I do not know where to start. Can you help?** Start by educating yourself with information based on an outline of your desires and goals in mind. READ.

6. **I weigh myself every day and I do not see where I am losing weight. Why?** The scale is probably the second sign that we have gained or loss weight. The first being our clothes, so often you find yourself jumping on that scale to help you qualify your efforts. I have fallen for this process myself. The fact is the scale cannot tell you if you have some unusual conditions going on. It cannot give you the account of your lean muscle and fat ratio (I know there are machine out there, that will perform this). I once jumped on one of those in a doctors office and it showed me as being 24% body fat. I knew and that doctor knew the results were false. I did my research

and found that if you are not hydrated you will receive an incorrect reading. By the way, I was 9% body fat. A scale causes you to think you have room to go out and eat a little extra when you know it's really not time. The list goes on. The best way is to find that outfit you just refuse to throw out and try it every now and then, along with your every day clothes. After all if you're healthy and your clothes fit nice the scale won't matter.

Closing comments by Victoria "Jazz"

Upon two weeks of your program start the process of your nutrition. I often express the importance of nutrition. I give it 90% of the program. Example, if you take a power lifter and give him a controlled eating plan, then take a body builder and allow him to eat whatever he likes, the difference will be surprising. The power lifter will show lean body mass whereas the body builder clearly will have no signs of being "cut."

SAMPLES OF PAIN AND PLEASURE REFERENCES

Pain References

How will this affect my...	POOR CHOICES AND OVEREATING FOODS
Relationship with God?	My witness will not be credible. I will not have the energy necessary to fulfill my purpose.
Relationship with Spouse?	My spouse will have to care for me because of health challenges. We will have no intimacy because of the impotence caused by some diseases. My spouse will probably be widowed. Another person will help him/her spend my insurance money.
Relationship with Children?	My children will eat the wrong foods or too much food because I modeled this behavior for them. I will not be available for them because of a lack of energy, sickness or death.
Health?	My health will be challenged. I will be fat. I will develop cancer, high blood pressure, strokes, impotence, diabetes, high cholesterol, or some other painful disease. I will die an early death.
Finances and Career	I will have to spend money to buy clothes in a larger size. I will have to spend money to buy medication and pay for doctor visits. My appearance may hinder my promotion on my job.

Pleasure References

How will this affect my...	DISCIPLINE IN FOOD CHOICES AND EATING
Relationship with God?	My witness will be credible. Trustworthiness and discipline will appear in other areas of my life. I will have the energy necessary to fulfill my purpose.
Relationship with Spouse?	My spouse will not have to care for me because of health challenges due to overeating. We can continue to be intimate as long as we want.
Relationship with Children?	My children will eat the right foods in proportion to their needs based on what has been modeled for them. I will have energy and the health necessary to be available for them.
Health?	I will not be fat. I will not develop the diseases that are caused by overeating. I will not eat my way into an early grave. If I lose 10 pounds, I can lengthen my life, lower my cholesterol and my blood pressure.
Finances and Career	I will not have to spend money to buy clothes in a larger size. I will not have to spend money to buy medication and pay for doctor visits. My appearance may not hinder my promotion on my job.

Pain References

How will this affect my...	PROCRASTINATION
Relationship with God?	I will not be obedient to God. I will not fulfill my purpose. God will have to give my assignment to a dependable other.
Relationship with Spouse?	My spouse will find me to be undependable.
Relationship with Children?	My children will find me to be undependable. My children will not be dependable because of what I modeled for them.
Health?	My health will be challenged if I put off doing what is necessary to remain healthy.
Finances and Career	I will miss opportunities for promotion. I will not receive the raises I could possibly get if I were dependable.

Pleasure References

How will this affect my…	NOT PROCRASTINATING
Relationship with God?	I will be obedient to God and do things in a timely manner. I will fulfill my purpose by prioritizing my work.
Relationship with Spouse?	My spouse will find me to be udependable and trustworthy.
Relationship with Children?	My children will find me to be dependable. My children will be dependable because of what I modeled for them.
Health?	My health will not be challenged because of me not caring for myself in a timely manner.
Finances and Career	I will not miss opportunities for promotion due to procrastination. I will receive the raises that are due me because I am dependable and I complete tasks in a timely manner. I will gain a competitive edge in business.

Pain References

How will this affect my...	OVER-SPENDING
Relationship with God?	I will not be available to do what God wants me to do if I am bound to creditors. I will not have money to obey God in the area of giving.
Relationship with Spouse?	I will have a bad relationship because of the stress caused by excessive bills. I will probably be divorced. My spouse will probably marry someone and give him or her the things I don't have.
Relationship with Children?	I will have to deny my children the things they need. My children will over-spend because I have modeled this behavior for them.
Health?	The stress of over-spending will cause my health to be challenged.
Finances and Career	I will have to live from paycheck to paycheck. I will not have the finances to save.

Pleasure References

How will this affect my...	DISCIPLINE IN SPENDING
Relationship with God?	I will be available to do what God wants me to do. I will be able to obey God in the area of giving.
Relationship with Spouse?	My spouse and I will be able to accumulate wealth and things together. We will be able to enjoy the work of our hands. We will be able to provide for our children's future.
Relationship with Children?	I will be able to provide the things my children need. My children will have a model of how to manage money.
Health?	The will be no stress because of over-spending.
Finances and Career	My business will prosper. I will not have to live from paycheck to paycheck. I will have the finances to save. I will be able to get the dream house, car, boat, etc. I desire.

Pain References

How will this affect my...	ANGER
Relationship with God?	I will not be in obedience to God's command. My flesh will be in control of my life, rather than the Spirit of God. I will not be the person I believe I am or could be. I will give misleading impressions of my character, commitment, and competence.
Relationship with Spouse?	My spouse will be afraid of me. My spouse will not be able to share information openly with me. My spouse will seek counsel from others, rather than me. My spouse will hide things from me.
Relationship with Children?	My children will be afraid of me. My children will not be able to share information openly with me. My children will avoid me.
Health?	My health will be challenged because of the chemicals released into my body during anger. I could develop high blood pressure, strokes, cancer, and other diseases.
Finances and Career	My business will suffer. I will not get promotions and raises. I will have to spend money on doctor visits and medication.

Pleasure References

How will this affect my...	ANGER MANAGEMENT
Relationship with God?	I will be in obedience to God's command. I can submit to the Spirit of God in my life. I will display character in keeping with who I am in God.
Relationship with Spouse?	My spouse will not be afraid of me. My spouse will be able to share information openly with me. My spouse will seek counsel from me, rather than others. My spouse will not seek to hide things from me.
Relationship with Children?	My children will not be afraid of me. My children will be able to share information openly with me. My children will want to be with me.
Health?	My health will not be challenged because of the chemicals that would be released into my body during anger.
Finances and Career	My business will not suffer because of anger. I will get promotions and raises. Money will come to me because I know how to win friends and influence people.

WORKBOOK SECTION

Understanding The Power of the Human Will

Understanding the will of man requires some simple insight into God's creative design for mankind. The Word of God is the primary source for explanations regarding the nature of mankind. The Bible explains how God designed the human mind and how we are to properly manage our human behavior and our interpersonal relationships. It is refreshing to know that God cared about man's mental and emotional well being enough to give insight into human behavior in advance of the emergence of the fields of psychiatry and psychology.

Key Statement: The will of man is the most dominant authority over human affairs in the earth.

The will of man is the primary factor in the control of human affairs and must be respected since God will not violate a man's will. God will not save a man against his will and Satan cannot make a person do anything against his will.

1. Man has been uniquely created as a tripartite being. What are those three parts?

   1.1____________________________________

   1.2____________________________________

   1.3____________________________________

2. Complete the following statements.

   2.1 ________________________ is what man is.

   2.2 The __________________is where man lives.

   2.3 The _______________is what man possesses.

3. There are five components to the soul. What are they?

   3.1____________________________________

   3.2____________________________________

   3.3____________________________________

   3.4____________________________________

   3.5____________________________________

4. We will do well in life (prosper) and be in health relative to the development of________________

5. The will of man controls what?

   5.1______________________________________

   5.2______________________________________

   5.3______________________________________

   5.4______________________________________

   5.5______________________________________

6. What will determine if a person will act upon the scriptural principles that are necessary for behavior change? ________________________________

7. Complete the following statements.

   7.1 Life is ____________________________driven.

   7.2 We live or we die by the_______that we make.

8. Who controls the establishment of one's will? ____

9. Since I have the power to change the criteria for believing, I am not a victim of_______________.

10. Change is always the product of _______________.

11. According to the Bible, the new birth is a spiritual transaction that changes what part of man? ______

12. When we put forth a sincere effort to change, we can be assured that our initiative ___________________

Choose from one of the following answers.

12.1 Will go unassisted

12.2 Changes automatically

12.3 Will not go unassisted

There is a wealth of knowledge concerning behavioral change in the Bible. I have used those principles to develop programs to minister to drug addicts; to those struggling with body weight, to couples dealing with marital problems, and to business poeple needing to overcome procrastination to gain the competitive edge in business. These principles have worked for others and they will work for you.

13. A person must set his or her will to follow certain principles to experience behavior change. What are the five principles?

13.1____

13.2____

13.3____

13.4____

13.5______________________________________

14. Accepting as fact that for which you have no sense realm evidence is called____________________.

15. What is the importance of faith?

15.1______________________________________

15.2______________________________________

16. How is faith released?__________________________

17. What is an affirmation?_________________________

18. What is a statement called that is in agreement with the Word of God regardless of what the situation suggests? ______________________________

19. Name the principle that says that those with whom we interact will have an impact on our success, either negatively or positively?

19.1______________________________________

20. Natural development is always accelerated through a ____________________________________example.

21. A ________________________is one who provides a visible natural example of that which is desired.

22. We should also model the ________________of successful others because principles work for anybody who will work them.

23. It is the Order of God to teach us and to train us by ____________________________________.

24. What principle best describes this statement being accountable for your action helps to anchor you in your resolve?____________________________

25. Where there is no ______________, there will be a greater opportunity to relapse and get off track.

Understanding the Will-Setting Process

Before you can take control of the will-setting process, you must understand how God engineered the process to work. ***Romans 7:23*** says, ***"But I see another law in my members, warring against the law of my mind…"*** The law of the mind implies that the mind functions in a certain way all the time. Since God is a God of order, He has engineered the mental complex of man to function in a consistent manner.

From the observations of scripture and life experiences, there are some outstanding truths that give us insight into how we function mentally and psychologically. The mind is the center of reasoning where deliberation of the issues of life takes place. This deliberative process has five components that ultimately impact the will of man. The will of man carries out the deliberation of the mind by instructing the body to behave based on the information that the mind has processed.

1. This decision process is influenced by five factors that you and I can take control of when we know how to do so. What are those five factors?

   1.1____________________________________

   1.2____________________________________

   1.3____________________________________

   1.4____________________________________

   1.5____________________________________

2. The quality of our lives is [2.1] by my thoughts, [2.2] by my choices, [2.3] by my words and [2.4] daily by my actions!

   2.1____________________________________

   2.2____________________________________

   2.3____________________________________

   2.4____________________________________

3. To bring the mental process under the authority of the Word of God is to bring our thought process in agreement with what?

   3.1____________________________________

4. The emotions that you experience during deliberation can ____________impact the outcome of your decision. Choose from one of the following answers.

   4.1 Negatively

   4.2 Positively

   4.3 Negatively or positively

5. The emotional track will run its course of feelings and behaviors unless I purposely and consciously do what [5.1] to give new direction for my emotions.

   5.1____________________________________

6. As neurological triggers, what do our emotions stimulate?

   6.1____________________________________

   6.2____________________________________

7. Name some effective ways of telling your emotions that you are in charge and that you will not let them run their course.

   7.1____________________________________

   7.2____________________________________

   7.3____________________________________

   7.4____________________________________

8. If you have established certain [8.1] for your life and purposely make decisions in agreement with those priorities, you will purposely set your will to your desired course.

   8.1____________________________________

9. The Master Reference Guide for decision-making which will cause you to do what?

   9.1____________________________________

10. As you increasingly define your purpose, what will you impact more and more?

    10.1___________________________________

11. The _________________ of significant others has a great influence on our decision making processes.

12. The two groups of significant others that will impact our decision-making are

    12.1_________________________________

    12.2_________________________________

13. When we select mentors and others to whom we will be accountable, we must be sure that their values are what?

    13.1_________________________________

14. The impact of _______________ is sufficient to help those in the support group to hold a course toward beneficial behavior.

15. What establishes the will of man?

    15.1_________________________________

16. The will is programmed to move away from [16.1] and toward [16.2].

    16.1_________________________________

    16.2_________________________________

17. Why are men presented the pain side of a poor decision?

    17.1____________________________________

18. The will functions in concert with deep-seated beliefs and values until what occurs?

    18.1____________________________________

19. Man is designed to make decisions at two levels. Describe each?

    19.1____________________________________

    19.2____________________________________

20. These decisions are made in agreement with what?

    20.1____________________________________

21. When we [21.1] the pleasurable benefit of a situation above the discomfort or pain caused by the situation, our will is established to endure the [21.2] to obtain the [21.3].

    21.1____________________________________

    21.2____________________________________

    21.3____________________________________

22. The Human Will makes [22.1], which when established forms a new behavior path.

    22.1________________________________

23. When pleasing God is the central object of my affections and my Christian witness is of critical importance, any situation, habit or temptation that challenges this commitment is perceived as __________________________________.

24. As I learn to associate pain with habits and misbehaviors that challenge my commitment to pleasing God and elevate the benefits of pleasing God, my will can be established to do two things. What are they?

    24.1________________________________

    24.2________________________________

The Practical Application of the Will Power Principles

1. Winning in the situations of life is a matter of the

    1.1________________________________

2. To apply any spiritual principle, there are four things that are required. What are they?

   2.1____

   2.2____

   2.3____

   2.4____

3. Developing and working your strategy requires following a simple step-by-step plan of action repetitiously until you get the desired results, just as assembling Christmas toys. What are the four things necessary?

   3.1____

   3.2____

   3.3____

   3.4____

4. What are the seven key statements about the function of the human will relative to human steps to Will Power Development?

   4.1____

4.2____

4.3____

4.4 Ask yourself these probing questions.

A) ______________________________________?

1.____?

2.____?

3.____?

4.____?

5.____?

B).______________________________________?

C) ______________________________________?

D) ______________________________________.

4.5____

4.6 ______________________________________.

4.7 ______________________________________.

ANSWER KEY

The Principles of Behavioral Change

1. Man has been uniquely created as a tripartite being. What are those three parts?

    1.1 Spirit

    1.2 Soul

    1.3 Body

2. Complete the following statements.

    2.1 Spirit is what man is.

    2.2 The body is where man lives.

    2.3 The soul is what man possesses.

3. There are five components of the soul. What are they?

    3.1 The mind

    3.2 The will

    3.3 The imagination

    3.4 The emotions

3.5 The intellect

4. We will do well in life (prosper) and be in health relative to the development of the soul.

5. The will of man controls what?

   5.1 The degree of obedience

   5.2 The level of believing

   5.3 The power fear has over us

   5.4 The consistency of our character

   5.5 The measure of blessing we enjoy in life

6. What will determine if a person will act upon the scriptural principles that are necessary for behavior change? A man's will

7. Complete the following statements.

   7.1 Life is choice driven.

   7.2 We live or we die by the choices that we make.

8. The establishing of the will is in whose control? Man

9. Since I have the power to change the criteria for believing, I am not a victim of how my will functions.

10. Change is always the product of human effort.

11. The new birth is a spiritual transaction that changes what part of man? the spirit of man

12. When we put forth the purposeful effort needed for change, we can be assured that our initiative will not go unassisted.

13. A person must set his or her will to follow certain principles to experience the results. What are the five principles?

    13.1 The principle of faith

    13.2 The principle of affirmation

    13.3 The principle of dominant influence

    13.4 The principle of modeling

    13.5 The principle of accountability

14. Accepting for fact that for which you have no sense realm evidence is biblical believing.

15. Why is faith important?

    15.1 It pleases God and He will reward those who diligently seek Him by faith.

15.2 All of the promises of God are received by faith.

15.3 You can overcome any situation by faith.

16. How is faith released? By the words of our mouths

17. What is an affirmation? A faith confession

18. A statement in agreement with what the Word of God says about a situation regardless of what it appears to be is what? A faith confession

19. Those who we interact with will have an impact on our success, either negatively or positively is what principle?

    19.1 The Principle of Dominate Influence

20. Natural development is always accelerated through a visible natural example.

21. A role model is one who provides a visible natural example of that which is desired.

22. We should also model the growth strategies of successful others because principles work for anybody who will work them.

23. It is the Order of God to teach us and to train us by examples.

24. Being accountable for your action helps to anchor you in your resolve is what principle? The Principle of Accountability

25. Where there is no accountability, there will be a greater opportunity to relapse and get off track.

Understanding the Will Setting Process

1. This decision process is influenced by five factors that you and I can take control of when we know how to do so. What are those five factors?

    1.1 The emotional state that you are in

    1.2 The questions that you choose to ask about the decision you are about to make

    1.3 The mentor references and accountability factors in your life

    1.4 The pain and pleasure reference we make during deliberation

    1.5 The values and beliefs that we have about the issues that are being deliberated

2. The quality of our lives is 2.1 by my thoughts, 2.2 by my choices, 2.3 by my words and 2.4 daily by my actions!

2.1 Conceived

2.2 Composed

2.3 Confirmed

2.4 Constructed

3. To bring the mental process under "the authority of the Word of God" is to bring our thought process in agreement with

    3.1 What God teaches us to do in the scriptures

4. The emotions that you experience during deliberation can 4.1 impact the outcome of your decision.

    4.1 Negatively

    4.2 Positively

    4.3 Negatively or positively

5. The emotional track will run its course of feelings and behavior unless I purposefully and consciously 5.1 to give new direction for my emotions

    5.1 Interrupt the process

6. Our emotions are neurological triggers that stimulate what? 6.2

    6.1 Certain behaviors

    6.2 Feelings

7. Name some effective ways of telling your emotions that you are in charge and that you will not let them run their course?

    7.1 Stop and take a deep breath

    7.2 Count to ten

    7.3 Make a positive affirmation

8. If you have established certain 8.1 for your life and purposefully make decisions in agreement with those priorities, you will purposefully set your will to your desired course.

    8.1 Non-negotiable priorities

9. The Master Reference Guide for decision-making will cause you to do what?

    9.1 Always choose in agreement with these priorities.

10. The more defined your purpose is, the more impact you will have in the deliberation process.

11. The perception of significant others has a great influence on our decision making processes.

12. The two groups of significant others that will impact our decision-making are

    12.1 Those who acceptance we need (friends, support groups, family, etc.)

    12.2 Those who we consider to be our mentors.

13. When we select mentors and others to which we will be accountable, we must be sure that their values are those that agree with the principles of scripture.

14. The impact of accountability is sufficient to help those in the support group to hold a course toward beneficial behavior.

15. What establishes the will of man?

    15.1 References to pain and pleasure

16. The will is programmed to move away from 16.1 and toward 16.2.

    16.1 Pain

    16.2 Pleasure

17. Why are men presented the pain side of a poor decision?

    17.1 To encourage man to make the decision toward the pleasure and profitable side

18. The will functions in concert with deep-seated beliefs and values until what?

    18.1 It is challenged by pain or pleasure

19. Man is designed to make decisions at two levels. What are they?

    19.1 Conscious level

    19.2 Subconscious level

20. These decisions are made in agreement with what?

    20.1 The beliefs and values that we have

21. When we 21.1 the pleasurable benefit of a situation above the discomfort or pain caused by the situation, our will is established to endure the 21.2 to obtain the 21.3.

    21.1 Elevate

    21.2 Short-term discomfort and pain

    21.3 Pleasurable benefit

22. The human will makes 22.1, which when established, forms a new behavior path.

    22.1 Small gradual concessions

23. When pleasing God is the central object of my affections and my Christian witness is of critical importance, any situation, habit or temptation that challenges this commitment is perceived as emotional pain.

24. As I learn to associate pain with the habits and misbehavior that challenge my commitment to pleasing God and elevate the benefits of pleasing God, my will can be established to do two things. What are they?

    24.1 Move away from the habit

24.2 Move toward pleasing God.

The Practical Application of the Will Power Principles

1. Winning in the situations of life is a matter of the

   1.1 Will

2. To apply any spiritual principle, there are four things that are required. What are they?

   2.1 First, you need a revelation of the principle, which is an understanding of the principle at the level of your comprehension.

   2.2 Secondly, you need a role model; you need to see the principle lived out in the lives of others.

   2.3 Thirdly, you need a regiment of faith, which is a systematic way to apply the principle that has yielded results for others and will yield results for you.

   2.4 Finally, you need a righteous resolve; this is a positive, beneficial, righteous reason for the success of this principle.

3. Developing and working your strategy requires following a simple step-by-step plan of action

repetitiously until you get the desired results, just as assembling Christmas toys. What are the four things necessary?

3.1 You will need a picture of the end results

3.2 You will need confidence in the assembly instructions

3.3 You will need the proper tools that are required for assembly

3.4 You will need to follow the instructions in a correct and systematic order

4. What are the seven key statements about the function of the human will relative to human steps to Will Power Development?

4.1 Complete the Master Reference Form.

4.2 Identify the habit you desire to break.

4.3 Repeat, *"I can do all things through the power of God which strengthens me"* ten times.

4.4 Ask yourself these probing questions.

A. How does this habit negatively effect my

1) Relationship with God?

2) Relationship with spouse (if married)?

3) Relationship with children and family?

4) Health?

5) Future income & career?

B. What profit will breaking this habit bring me?

C. Who do I know who has overcome a similar habit?

D. Who could support me in my effort to change?

4.5 Locate Pain Reference Enhancers. Find photos, books or video documentaries on the painful consequences of this habit.

4.6 Formulate pain and pleasure affirmation. Write it down and say it as a conscious interrupt to the habitual behavior.

4.7 Call a friend and caring others to tell them about your decision.

The *Will* to *Win*

MASTER REFERENCE GUIDE

PRIORITY	OBJECTIVE	PURPOSE (Why is this important to you?)

Pain References

How will this affect my...	
Relationship with God?	
Relationship with Spouse?	
Relationship with Children?	
Health?	
Finances and Career	

Pleasure References

How will this affect my…	
Relationship with God?	
Relationship with Spouse?	
Relationship with Children?	
Health?	
Finances and Career	

Pain References

How will this affect my…	
Relationship with God?	
Relationship with Spouse?	
Relationship with Children?	
Health?	
Finances and Career	

Pleasure References

How will this affect my…	
Relationship with God?	
Relationship with Spouse?	
Relationship with Children?	
Health?	
Finances and Career	

NOTES

NOTES

NOTES